About the Author

DAVID SPURR was born in Princeton, New Jersey. He attended the University of Michigan, where he received his Ph.D. in comparative literature in 1978. From 1971 to 1973 he worked as a staff correspondent for United Press International in France and in Eastern Europe. His publications include articles on modern and comparative literature as well as journalistic pieces on a variety of subjects. He is currently assistant professor of English at the University of Illinois at Chicago.

YELLOW EARTH, GREEN JADE
Constants in Chinese Political Mores

HARVARD STUDIES
IN INTERNATIONAL AFFAIRS
Number 41

YELLOW EARTH, GREEN JADE

Constants in Chinese Political Mores

by Simon de Beaufort

Foreword by John K. Fairbank

Published by the
Center for International Affairs
Harvard University

Harvard University
Center for International Affairs

Executive Committee

Created in 1958, the Center for International Affairs fosters advanced study of basic world problems by scholars from various disciplines and senior officials from many countries. The research of the Center focuses on economic, social, and political development; the management of force in the modern world; the problems and relations of advanced industrial societies; transnational processes and international order; and technology and international affairs.

The Harvard Studies in International Affairs, which are listed at the back of this book, may be ordered from the Publications Office, Center for International Affairs, 1737 Cambridge St., Cambridge, Mass. 02138, at the prices indicated. Recent books written under the auspices of the Center, listed on the last pages, may be obtained from bookstores or ordered directly from the publishers.

About the Author_____

Under a different name, Simon de Beaufort has lived in China and dealt with officialdom there. A student of Chinese affairs since the mid-fifties, he has practiced what some people like to call Dragonology from the fringes of China's cultural sphere as well as from inside the People's Republic at some of the crucial junctures in the Communist regime's history.

ACKNOWLEDGEMENTS

This book owes much to the pertinent and thoughtful suggestions offered by Professors John K. Fairbank, Edwin O. Reischauer, and Benjamin I. Schwartz. The work also greatly benefited from the help given by Dr. Benjamin H. Brown, of the Center for International Affairs, Harvard University, Dr. Nancy M. Viviani, of the Australian National University, and Mr. Peter Jacobsohn, Editor of Publications of the Center. Finally, I wish to express my gratitude to Mrs. Eva Morvay for having tirelessly deciphered the manuscript.

CONTENTS

PREFACE

China is made more mysterious by those who study it. Some profess political science and find things new and strange. Some are historians who by nature stress continuities. Liberated women find Chinese women liberated. Tourists find the service excellent. Journalists have trouble. Who will see China whole?

The writer of this study obviously is acquainted with the academic disciplines and also with Chinese ideals and realities and the gaps between them all. He has read the books but also dealt with the officials. Contradictions do not surprise him. He seeks no single or simple explanation. His key to understanding China is the sense of political style, a style different from that of outsiders in the West, a style that has had a long time developing and does not quickly change. It is something one senses in Chinese behavior and sees in Chinese history, and he does not try to clothe it in the academic fig-leaf of "political culture."

Plainly, the writer's objectivity toward Chinese behavior is informed by a considerable grasp of Western ways as well as Chinese. He has been around long enough, but is still young enough, to see things in an historical and cultural perspective but with fresh eyes. In his title, the "Yellow Earth" stands for the Chinese common people. "Green Jade" represents the ruling class. Both have been there since the dawn of history. Neither will soon disappear.

John K. Fairbank
Francis Lee Higginson Professor of History, Emeritus
Harvard University

INTRODUCTION

Paris' "new philosophers" have recently proclaimed the demise of the "Chinese myth." This phrase is yet another indication, among the intelligentsia of the West, of a shift from the tendency to ascribe to the regime established in 1949 in Peking as high a place in political thinking as that enjoyed by the Chinese Empire in the eyes of the *philosophes* of the Enlightenment.

The passing of an intellectual fashion would perhaps not greatly matter if it concerned a minute tribe in an isolated corner of the world or some unprepossessing and all but forgotten culture of the distant past. But as it bears on foreign perceptions of humanity's oldest living civilization and most populous nation, it raises at once some interesting questions.

The set of pious clichés which until recently had been so commonly accepted as facts regarding "Maoist" China is now more and more easily discarded. To quite a few of the French "new gurus" for instance, the outcome of the succession struggle in Peking after Mao's death has opened new vistas. It has provided them with the revelation that people they considered traitorous and unworthy (Hua Kuofeng and his allies) could accede to power in the People's Republic instead of the "left," which the "Gang of Four" had seemed to represent so successfully; that for long there had surely been something rotten in the Middle Kingdom; that testimonies such as those of Pasqualini[1] or Simon Leys,[2] misguided as their authors may have appeared at first, must have contained disturbingly accurate elements of information. For all the agonizing reappraisal this entails, one does not feel one is about to cease dealing with a semi-mythical China. On the contrary, one has the impression that a new set of clichés is in the making, that it will bear the hallmarks of disillusion and superficiality, and that it will contribute little—or even do violence—to common wisdom regarding a country that is possibly seen today in not much clearer terms than the nation the Manchu dynasty governed two centuries ago. What was, however, excusable in the 18th century is not acceptable today. Utopian fantasies barely related to the past and present history of China must at long last give way to a more modest and factual assessment.

*   *   *

When attempting to describe the exoticism of Chinese society and the extraordinarily secretive regime that rules it, there is something to be said for starting with the banal question frequently heard when various Western or Western-oriented governments were in the process of establishing formal relations with "Red China": was that regime first and foremost "Communist" or "Chinese"? The basic answer was of course contained in the question: the People's Republic established in 1949 in Peking was both, depending on the period and the leadership group under discussion.

And yet, the question had its virtues. On further examination it appeared that the Chinese Communist Party and its leading theorists had always displayed a fascination with Lenin's dialectics on political struggle and the seizure of power, and that they had always referred both explicitly and implicitly to Stalin's experiences in building the Soviet Union's party and state apparatus, and in transforming Russian society. On the other hand, the persistence of national idiosyncracies in China's Communist leaders was equally striking: the new rulers harped on ancient historical precedents in a way not dissimilar to that of the Emperors; like their predecessors on the Dragon's throne, they handed down to the people moral maxims encapsulated in short groups of ideograms that were balanced in form and content; Mao's writings contained as many references to Confucian treatises as to Stalin's dissertations; "Taoist" influences, possibly through the teachings of Sun Tzu, the fabled strategist of the Sixth century B.C., permeated Mao's military thinking; and in the 70s, one form of political recognition for a leader—Mao, as well as others—who had achieved national eminence, still consisted in publicizing samples of his calligraphy.

True, the new regime saw itself as breaking away from the decadent and abhorred history of the past century; as not merely opening a new and auspicious chapter in the traditional succession of cycles of order and chaos, but as entering a momentous stage in the ascending spiral which, from the peasant rebellions of the past to the future transformations of Chinese society, would ultimately bring about communism in China. But the political mores now prevailing in China suggest a far more complex picture in which sweeping and radical revolutionary changes coexist with remarkably resilient native patterns of social and political behavior. Some of these latter constants, it is hoped, will be illustrated in what follows.

THE MASSES, THE DRAGON'S THRONE, AND THE MANDARINS

Touring China and observing the everyday life of its people, one might be forgiven for thinking of the old Greek grammar example of the collective singular: *Ta zoa trekei*.[3] Those who do not have firsthand experience of the Chinese landscape will find it profitable to sit through Joris Ivens' twelve-hour cinematographic fresco of contemporary China ("How Yukung Moved Mountains"): its imagery conveys quite forcefully to the outsider a notion of how truly massive Chinese "masses" are and how uniform their attitudes appear to be most of the time.

Early visitors to the People's Republic—particularly "old China hands"—used to speak darkly of the "blue ants" who had displaced since 1949 the erstwhile fun-loving, mercurial, individualistic Chinese they knew (*"they* have changed *my* Chinese"). And to be sure, since 1949 the Chinese people have gone through various stages of regimentation such as they had not known for a long time.

Other factors aggravated this feeling of estrangement: a puritan curtailment of visible social inequalities provided the trappings for an austere and dignified environment, while the gradual pauperization of all forms of cultural life put a stop to the renaissance which followed the fall of the Empire in 1911.

These elements tended to obscure the rest of the picture.

"Masses" in China had long deserved that appellation to an
extent possibly unmatched anywhere else. This was due to
historical reasons which still persist today and will most
probably remain a constant in the foreseeable future. As is
well known, the Chinese are a predominantly agricultural
people. In this vast country high-density populations with
severely limited tillable land at their disposal have organized
their social and political existence around a very intensive
gardening type of food-crop raising. The manpower
involved is huge; its physical concentration impressive. The
paddy-fields of Kwangtung with their leopard skin dotting
of big villages, or across the country, the communal
organization of rural chores with people in their hundreds
and thousands spreading manure or watering young shoots
literally by hand, are but two illustrations of the constraints
within which the Chinese live and work today as yesterday.
These basic patterns are there to stay for at least the next
generation, if Peking adheres to its present policy of coping
with these demographic pressures through the development
of small and medium-sized rural industries and the injection
of technological and scientific innovations into existing
agricultural techniques.

   In this particular framework, the individual tends to see
himself not as one of a group, but rather as part of a vastly
ramified mechanism extending—if his intellectual horizon is
wide enough—to the limits of the civilized world (which still
more often than not coincide with those of China).
Individual values—as opposed to communal ones—are not
absent, far from it. Indeed, past the first few years of one's
existence, they will frequently be tested to the utmost. What
is virtually missing, even today, after close to a century of
exposure to foreign creeds and terminologies, is the notion
of citizenship, and the preoccupation with personal rights
which it entails. That particularly martial brand of

revolution which triumphed in 1949, has not produced a Chinese equivalent of the soldier-citizen born in the French Revolution.[4] As the "good little soldier" Lei Feng, a Maoist hero, used to put it: "I am but a tiny screw" (in the mechanism of the new Chinese society).

Language, at its most colloquial, has long reflected these traits. Where the English would say "everybody" or "everyone" the Chinese will use the expression "ta chia," literally meaning "the great family" and by extension "all people." There is, however, no linguistic barrier to the rendering of "everyone"; it is simply that Chinese equivalents imply a will to differentiate. It is interesting to note that the Communist Party addresses the masses collectively ("the revolutionary masses," "the wide masses," "the wide masses of our army and people," "the revolutionary masses of our multinational people,"), while tending to speak of its membership and cadres on a far more individualized plane ("full-fledged members of the CCP at every level, and especially leading cadres,..."). To this, the masses seem to respond, with the blessings of officialdom, by the continual recourse to expressions emphasizing their collectiveness: for instance, a collective form of the first person plural pronoun ("tsa men"); or to designate the people at large, the phrase "the one hundred (good old) family names" ("Lao Pai Hsing"—a reference to the ancient clan names which still today provide the only source of family identification). It is probably symptomatic that the *People's Daily* (November 15, 1977) should choose to illustrate the ravages of anarchist tendencies in a young worker by quoting him as saying: "I am master of my own ship after God" (*"Tien shih lao ta, wo shih lao eul"*), which in the West would be taken as indicative of an obstreperous but possibly healthy disposition to individual enterprise.

*   *   *

Chinese trains have their own internal radio which is in the charge of young women. These guardian angels combine the duties of a disc-jockey and a catechist. Besides providing passengers with light music—in the veins and quotas officially approved—and practical advice, they dispense generous portions of the Gospel of the day, as well as ad hoc exhortations.

Approaching Peking, one will regularly be gratified by triumphant paeans extolling the capital city of China. With religious fervor, the ancient and recent past of Peking, its role as the tabernacle of central authority, its sacredness as Chairman Mao's monstrance, are emphasized in terms carefully designed to equate the place and its function as the abode of the Great Leader. "All hearts are turning toward Peking," reiterate countless hymns, because this is where rises the "red sun" (or in the less restrained times of the Cultural Revolution "the reddest, reddest, red sun in our hearts"), in other words Mao Tse-tung. Admittedly, Chairman Mao was not the first leader in human history to be compared to the sun; Peking is not the first and only capital to be exalted with such lyricism. What is remarkable in the Chinese case is the way its present praise links up with the most ancient roots of native political tradition, so much so in fact that the rhetoric involved seems to reflect far more than a nationalistic urge to affirm the prestige of the seat of central government. One is dealing here with a cosmogonic locus: the true center of China—it is always from the capital city that emanates the civilizing influence which ultimately will extend to the confines of the world. As such, it is the hallowed, and only possible, residence of the ruler of China;

the place and the man are one in forming the pivot of national unity, as well as that of true civilization.

The train ritual takes on its full significance when placed in the ceremonial context of central rule in China. The ruler in his capital city, the imperial court or the "center," must be seen to fill correctly their symbolic functions, and so to convey the necessary sentiment of permanence. One is tempted here to say that, while the Soviet leadership had been showing an increasing thirst for bourgeois respectability, its Chinese counterpart would seem to betray more august preoccupations.

*   *   *

Like other nations, the Chinese people have long displayed ambivalent attitudes towards their rulers. Basically, the latter are expected to show the minimum of organizational virtues which will make regular food-crop cultivation possible. In the absence of natural or man-made calamities— and provided it performs its symbolic functions—a weak central authority will receive the deferential "filial" treatment stronger regimes outside of China would find necessary to demand forcibly. The Chinese peasantry has shown and still seems to show a marked preference for a distant relationship with government: without going as far as Burmese peasants who equate it with flood and fire, the Chinese have long found virtue in the less militant holders of power. This does not detract from the vital character of the role ascribed to the supreme ruler or leader: he is and must remain a life-giving unifier, or in other words, the man capable through presence, example, suasion or action, of maintaining in a normal state of repair the social organization that ensures the livelihood of the Chinese people.

This notion was amply illustrated in the official literature of the People's Republic in 1976-77, after the downfall of the "Gang of Four." Part of the hagiography then devoted to the supreme leaders of the Chinese Communist Party eulogized their role (far more, it should be noted, than the Party's) in the all-important field of hydraulics. In the same way as the first semi-mythical Emperors, Mao Tse-tung was credited with issuing the quasi-magical instructions which, if followed, would bring permanent prosperity to the masses: "Harness the Yellow river," "Tame the Huai river." Chou En-lai, much like those sovereigns in the great dynasties who had proved their worth by correctly implementing the outlines of conduct established by their semi-mythical pre-decessors, was depicted as organizing the masses in a judicious succession of canal-digging and dam-raising activities. As to Hua Kuo-feng—the new Chairman of the Party—the mettle and ability he had shown at the provincial level had provided proof that he would be a worthy successor to both Mao and Chou. The Shaoshan irrigation project he had directed in Hunan had brought "the water of happiness," as peasants of 83 communes could attest today; he had himself quite fittingly described the main aqueduct in a calligraphy which now adorns its top in huge characters as a "river in the sky."

What is expected of central authority is thus in a sense minimal. Parts of Chinese elites traditionally saw, as people elsewhere have done, proof of a dynasty's legitimacy in its capacity to endure for a long period of time. Since the first unification of China, however, popular perceptions seem to have been quite different. For the masses, legitimacy is equated with the type of efficiency which has been described above. Rulers who cease to display the basic abilities expected of them are not redeemable: they are no longer in harmony with the natural order of things, as is soon proved by diverse calamities (and to be sure, in politically troubled times, canals will not be dredged and will overflow, and populations—that of Tang-Shan in 1976, for instance—will not be warned in time of impending earthquakes).

When disaster strikes across the land, therefore, confirming suspicions that the holder of supreme power has lost his right to occupy the dragon's throne, revolt is not only justified but legitimate, and indeed instrumental—in numerous instances, through peasant rebellions—in bringing to power a new dynasty. When one hears today an old Chinese woman using such expressions as: "I have known three dynasties; this one is by far the best," one cannot help thinking that in a way it exemplifies the basic attitudes of the people towards their rulers. But a more convincing illustration can probably be found in the behavior of the Peking press in the weeks following the death of Mao Tse-tung, when it took pains to rebuke all those who, with or without criminal intent, were spreading the rumor that the many natural disasters which had preceded the Chairman's demise heralded a change of regime. It is not without interest that the "Gang of Four" was later alleged by the same press to have—if only jokingly—attributed a similar meaning to those "signs." One has here a striking example of the resilience of "superstitions" which go a long way towards explaining the particular ambivalence basic to the relationship between the leaders and the led in China.

*   *   *

The West has long been fascinated by Chinese bureaucracy. Its levels of intellectuality, the extent to which it was relied upon by the sovereigns and accepted by the masses, were seen, quite justifiably, as unique features. The notions underlying the Chinese tradition of bureaucratic rule provided nourishment to vital Western trends of thought in the 18th century: the beliefs in man's perfectibility and in the state's right to intervene in fostering it were seen as having been vindicated by millennia of Chinese history.

This was of course only one side of the coin. Mandarins, the mandarinate, also became bywords of nepotism, symbols of a privileged class of intellectuals exercising a monopoly on state power. The terms came to be applied with great frequency to diverse groups in Western societies, with predictable emphasis on civil servants.

Two of these groups could conceivably be thought of as coming closest to Chinese traditional concepts of the character and role of a bureaucrat. One is the now defunct Indian Civil Service. Here one had a fairly long and well-established line of state functionaries with remarkable academic standards and sweeping powers in the local and central administration of the British Raj; these men, although not immune to varied forms of corruption, showed, by all accounts, a commendable sense of duty to the Empire as well as to its Indian subjects. However, they were colonial administrators, and the locally recruited among them remained, in the final analysis, servants of foreign masters. Moreover, to the very end their rule implied a wide range of different forms of coexistence with a motley assortment of agents for native political and administrative institutions.

The French Civil Service under the Fifth Republic offers another and possibly more fertile ground for comparison. While civil servants under the Third and Fourth Republics appeared to be content with providing permanent safeguards which would ensure that the state would not suffer overly from the zig-zags of politicians' politics, since 1958 the higher echelons of the Civil Service have provided a rising and by now very large number of power-sharers in both the Legislative and the Executive. This phenomenon has been explained mainly by two factors: the strong popular distrust of professional politicians which was quite evidently instrumental in the downfall of the Fourth Republic; and the increasing technical complexity of the issues facing modern statesmen.

The accession to political authority of a large number of civil servants has undoubtedly increased the meritocratic elements in French society and brought it nearer, in a sense, to a "mandarin" society. The differences between it and the Chinese model are, however, immense. The French official turned politician or statesman becomes one of the actors in parliamentary politics. His new environment has none of the homogeneity which by and large characterized the Chinese body politic[5]. He shares power with representatives of other groups who will try to reduce to their advantage his influence and numerical strength in state councils. A comeback in public favor of professional politicians, a "new wave" of young advocates of local interests, are hypotheses which in the present French context, he cannot dismiss once and for all.

If one now turns to the Chinese bureaucracy of today, it would seem only rational to seek out first its similarities with the Soviet model. After all, when Mao Tse-tung, Chou En-lai, Kang Sheng and others in Yenan forged a regular Communist Party out of the Red Army, they followed Leninist precepts and Soviet precedents. The Party and State apparatus which gradually came into being in China from 1949 onwards was closely inspired by Russian examples.

Bolshevik *aparatchiki*, it will be remembered, had lost no time in rediscovering the ways of Tsarist bureaucracy; in a similar fashion the new Chinese leadership was to trade the

egalitarian spirit of Yenan for hierarchic delights, drawing
on both Russian and indigenous recipes. References in
popular parlance to the new apparatus as a multi-storied
"Pagoda" linked it implicitly to the mandarin system;
the People's Liberation Army, *horresco referens*, was
ludicrously adorned with a batch of Marshals in resplendent
Russian-style uniforms; other examples of this swift and
profound transformation into a highly hierarchical machine
of power are legion.

With insignia and rank came precisely graded material
privileges: private residences ranging, by the austere
standards of the regime, from the comfortable cottage
allotted to the cadre of a rural district, to the exceptionally
luxurious bungalow of a national "leader"; exclusive means
of transportation (limousines, train sleepers of "Orient
Express" class, special planes); for officials on tour
(particularly ranking army officers), circuit houses whose
comforts make Indian equivalents in the days of the British
Raj look definitely restrained; personal staff, including
orderlies attached to individual officers in the Army. What
the Chinese press has recently printed concerning the
respective life-styles of Mao Tse-tung and Chou En-lai, on
the one hand, and of Chiang Ch'ing or Wang Hung-wen
of the "Gang of Four," on the other, has been corroborated
in part by independent evidence. There are leaders at the
apex of the Chinese hierarchy who elect to deny themselves
many of the special amenities made available to them and
who permanently adhere to a "proletarian" way of life,
whether by personal inclination (Mao) or deliberate choice
(Chou); there are others who quite naturally make the
perquisites their own, as Roxane Witke[6] was able to observe
as the guest of Chiang Ch'ing in Canton, and as other foreign
visitors have witnessed in the case of Wang Hung-wen in
Shanghai.

Indeed, by itself, the literature recurrently published in China to exhort Party cadres to strive for a frugal and simple life-style suggests that a trend towards self-indulgence, in spite of all efforts to the contrary, has predominated since the founding of the People's Republic. One cannot fail to be impressed, for instance, by the list of bad habits recently identified at the lower levels of the Party apparatus: rural administrators who need to be told (by means of disseminating across the country "resolutions" adopted by this or that party committee at brigade, commune, or district level) that they should not equate promotion with better accommodation and ought to stop expecting the populace to provide them with banquets on every tour of every part of their constituencies, or that they could dispense with carpets and sofas in their own offices—such administrators hardly look like the spearhead of a mighty revolutionary force on the march.

These privileges are part of the system which sees to it that they are not contested outside of the Party. In fact, apart from brief spurts of questioning during the Hundred Flowers crisis and the Cultural Revolution, one only comes across isolated instances of more or less disguised criticism (such as a wall newspaper appearing for a few days in June 1977 in one of the Peking universities). Only the abuse, not the use, of perquisites attracts from time to time a word of authorized reprimand. This was well illustrated when Chiang Ch'ing was berated for a comportment carefully emphasized as extravagant: closing permanently a public park in Peking to be able to ride horses at her leisure, or forbidding military aircraft to take off from a nearby airport when she spent the night in a pavilion of the Summer Palace.

For all purposes, holders of privileges attached to an official position may consider them as their rightful and undisputed possession. Among others, there remains an unforgettable image from the days when the Cultural Revolution actually meant popular upheaval and an uncertain future for practically any member of the party and state apparatus: the sight of very ancient functionaries crossing the teeming mobs gathered in the streets of Peking in the comfort of their silk-curtained limousines; eyes half-closed, their frail bodies carefully reclined on the grey cushions of the "Shanghai" or "Red Flag" carrying them, they seemed totally oblivious of the boisterous youths outside, as if the "serve the people" (*"wei jenmin fuwu"*) motto painted in Chairman Mao's calligraphy across the rear of their cars had been a talisman providing all necessary protection.

This, however, is only the surface of things. Privileges are far more enmeshed in the social fabric; for one thing, they tend to be hereditary. Private property is not what matters here. Indeed, whereas individual ownership of one's own living quarters is often seen elsewhere as symbolic of access to middle class status, under the present Chinese regime, the peasant and the worker will in many cases be encouraged to preserve or to acquire private ownership of his cottage or apartment, and to pass the property on to his descendants. The reasons for this are practical: although compressed to a minimum, expenses incurred in building additional housing for a steadily growing population are regarded by Chinese planners as a budgetary burden of such magnitude as to make it desirable to transfer whenever materially and politically possible to private persons the ownership and therefore the maintenance of their lodgings. The bureaucrat falls in a different category. He is already provided with living quarters which more often than not will be better than anything he could hope to acquire personally. He is aware in an egalitarian and puritanistic society of the perils attending the possession of art objects or luxuries clearly beyond the common citizen's reach. He will therefore be content with using, or abusing, the perquisites attached to his official position.

But what puts him and his close dependents in a different class altogether is access to exclusive information and learning. News in China is disseminated through two parallel channels. One is that of the national and provincial press and radio network whose services are offered to, and imposed on, the general public. These organs are really used as vehicles for political and ideological sermons. A prudently filtered and measured dose of information will be injected not for the sake of informing but for that of illustrating; the product is highly stereotyped and will undergo few local variations across the whole of China. The other channel belongs to the Communist Party: carefully graded information on both internal and external developments is broadcast through a diversity of bulletins, newsletters, and circulars; permanent procedures ensure, quite effectively, it seems, that each stratum of the party and state apparatus will only receive what it is entitled to. On the whole, Chinese bureaucrats are provided with adequate means to keep abreast of the situation outside their own country; more importantly, and in degrees varying with tensions at the top of the hierarchy as well as with their own official rank and position, they have access to data and analyses bearing on the internal situation which are permanently denied to their parishioners.

To be sure, near-eradication of illiteracy is a signal achievement of the People's Republic. But, just as in Imperial China education and high culture for the happy few meant privileged access to political power, information today plays a comparable role in the processes of cooptation and selection which regulate Chinese political life.

Volumes have been written in the West on the advantages

enjoyed by the aspirant to higher learning whose family background happens to be that of the professions, the upper echelons of the civil service, the managerial class, etc. Quite apart from nepotistical or social reflexes, the intellectual milieu surrounding childhood and adolescence makes now well-known differences. Children of Chinese cadre families not only benefit from such advantages in comparison to students of "worker-peasant-soldier" extraction, whatever the official efforts to promote the politically conscious and the meritorious in these less privileged strata of society; the scions of members of the ruling apparatus also enjoy the added advantage, when applying for admission to a given university or institute, of being quite alone in their intellectual class, in the sense that potential competitors from among the descendants of former bourgeois families are still commonly prevented from entering establishments of higher learning. Chinese cadres will therefore, quite naturally, send their children to the places—prestigious universities, Party schools—which will provide them with the best means to make a career in the apparatus and a comfortable living.

As for the Army, it seems to have its own, complete educational network, from nursery school to military academy; a general's son should find it comparatively easy to follow in his father's footsteps, if he and his father so wish. The inclination of the cadre class to perpetuate itself now seems deeply entrenched, if one goes by the episodic and half-hearted campaigns of the national press to publicize examples of different attitudes. For instance, military cadres of an army command in Shantung may be described in the midst of an effort to convince their own children of the superior merits of a life spent as an "ordinary" worker or peasant in the "service of the people." In other words, representatives of a very privileged social group are seen exhorting their offspring to forsake the comforts of their present life as well as the promises which higher studies hold for them, and to volunteer to be sent to more or less remote and backward parts of the countryside, never knowing precisely when they will be allowed to come back. The story will be true; the actors will have performed their parts with varying degrees of conviction; what is usually missing is a convincing statistical account of the movement's results. Instances are cited from time to time of a cadre performing successfully that sort of ritual, but they do seem to be isolated cases.

This impression is strengthened when one looks at the description of Mao Tse-tung's and Hua Kuo-feng's attitudes in such matters. The "proletarian" virtues they have both demonstrated in their relationship to their own children by having them go and "learn from the masses" are emphasized to a point where it becomes indirectly evident (considering the secrecy surrounding the leaders' private lives) that this is not a common trait among the ruling class.

It is worth remembering that by "bombarding headquarters," (i.e. subjecting the authorities to criticism) the Cultural Revolution activists were aiming both at power-holders and the monopolies enjoyed by the new mandarinate. They tried to control and restrict the exercise of official authority through systematic surveillance of the various echelons of the apparatus. They attempted to liberate information, the Red Guard newspapers regarding it as their mission to tell all on past and present topics. They sought to put an end to the elitist and technically very traditional forms of higher education then prevailing in the People's Republic. Their efforts were short-lived, except in the field of education where for ten years diverse radical formulas were tried with indifferent success (open universities, workers' universities, "worker-peasant-soldier" students, etc.). As late as 1975 this domain provided the arena for the "radical" wing to launch its last attack on the establishment as incarnated in the person of Teng Hsiao-ping. It was only after Mao Tse-tung's death and the ultimate failure of the "Shanghai group" (the "Gang of Four") that there was a gradual return to former standards in education.

Mao's deeply ingrained suspicions of mandarin bureaucrats and academic elites, the extraordinary response which the expression of these suspicions met among the youth during the Cultural Revolution, were all to be officially forgotten when in August 1977, at the Eleventh Party Congress, Hua Kuo-feng proclaimed the "end" of the Cultural Revolution and, a few weeks later, presided over the formal reopening of the central Party school which had been closed down during the Cultural Revolution. Once more in China the concept of a strong centralized state relying on an ideologically and socially homogenous bureaucracy appeared to have prevailed.

At this point, it is perhaps worth noting that one is not concerned here with assessing the moral fiber of the contemporary Chinese bureaucratic class. Present orthodoxy in Peking has it that only "a handful of capitalist-roaders" somehow disfigure a "great and glorious" Communist Party; one is requested to reject the thesis of the now disgraced "Shanghai Group" who claimed to have identified a full-fledged and menacing "bourgeoisie within the Party." A differing and conflicting analysis can also be made, with similar justification, in the case of past Confucian or neo-Confucian bureaucracies in China. After all, did they not harbor at practically any given time a rather motley crowd of statesmen and buffoons, sceptics and martyrs, cynics and idealists, quietists and Jansenists? What is significant here is the role which a distinct type of bureaucracy has, with extraordinary permanence, played in China until the end of the Empire and, in a new guise, after a long chaotic interlude, again since 1949.

*   *   *

"Democratic centralism" is a useful phrase when one grapples with the notions underlying Chinese political life. The expression may look unfortunate, a misnomer when applied to various forms of authoritarian rule. In fact, it is a useful code which only requires a modicum of deciphering.

Since October 1976, that is, since the downfall of the "Gang of Four," the new Chinese leadership (Hua Kuo-feng, Teng Hsiao-ping, *et alii*) has brought back to life and frequent usage the phrase in question. Very much part of the old Communist phraseological stock, "democratic centralism" was quite suddenly bandied about in contexts which implied a definite departure from the political situation China had known for the past few years. Because promises were made in the same breath of a "democratic atmosphere" in which expressions of opinion and dissent would be deemed a normal activity on the part of the average citizen or party member, many outside China thought they detected a "wind of liberalization" blowing in the People's Republic. Was not the regime announcing a "new spring" in the domain of culture to artists and writers who, it was officially recognized, had so badly suffered under the "fascist rule" of the so-called radical wing of the Party.

This, in fact, was quite beside the point. After "ten years of Cultural Revolution," the new team at the helm in

Peking was concerned with putting China's house in order
and the nation back to work. It wanted to infuse a new
sense of confidence and, if possible, of dedication both in the
masses and the Party membership; quite pragmatically,
it felt the need to enlist the support of cultural elites who, for
all purposes, had retired long ago into their tents. What the
leadership meant when it emphasized its attachment to
"democratic centralism," was a return to law and order
across the country, and as far as the Communist cadre was
concerned, the offer of a new deal. The leaders had put a
successful end to the war of succession; they would see to it
that the Party status and traditions protecting its membership from abuse and misuse of authority would from now on
be respected; in exchange, every Party member would be
expected to contribute to the restoration of a strong,
centralized, and "unified" hierarchy. In a sense, this was
simply another case of a party built on Leninist lines
struggling to put to the best possible use the internal
dynamics of this particular type of organization.

But one must go further in the decoding of the Chinese use
of the expression "democratic centralism." The sheer size of
the People's Republic, and of its population, the way this
land is infinitely segmented because of its weak com-
munications infrastructure, raise problems of government
and administration which have again and again been solved
—or sought to be solved—through seemingly contradictory
formulas. One finds a combination of extreme concentration of central authority in a very small number of hands,
and of remarkably widespread delegation of authority
to the local echelons of the apparatus.

Under the present regime, the power to assign and demote
officials as well as that of controlling ideology is the
prerogative of a group of people very often not exceeding a
dozen persons or less: the Party chairman and those

members of the Politburo who are not incapacitated by age, illness, political disgrace or their purely symbolic presence at the top of the hierarchy. The parallel deserves to be made with the Emperors and the inner circle of their entourage: councillors, censors, high ministers, favorites, empresses or eunuchs; in fact, it is at times noticeably explicit in the material produced, with official blessings, in criticism of the "Gang of Four" by Chinese pamphleteers and cartoonists. The power-holders at the imperial court looked on their rights regarding the bureaucracy and the reigning orthodoxy as their exclusive preserve; so do their successors in the Forbidden City.

Chinese novels in the past were replete with examples of the migratory nature of a state functionary's career. In *Six Chapters of a Floating Life,*[7] for instance, one comes to appreciate the uncertainties of a Chinese official's life which could be spent for a good part shuttling from one end of the vast Empire to the other. In a similar way, for reasons related either to administrative expediency or political prudence, when not both, the central authority in Peking today will provide civilian and military cadres with variegated careers. Films made in the People's Republic (for instance, the recent "Breaking Off," which recounts the founding of the first "Communist university" in South-East China) provide numerous illustrations of how officials coming from very different and sometimes very remote postings are "parachuted" into new assignments. (In the film cited, the cadre entrusted with the task of creating single-handedly the "Communist University" has been plucked without warning from his previous assignment as Party secretary of a rural district). At another level, the way Peking in 1974 re-assigned at one stroke practically all the chiefs of the Great Military Regions, at a time when they seemed to wield unparallelled power, was more than reminiscent of the techniques of government evolved by Imperial authority in the past.

Total concentration of power is perhaps even more evident in the realm of ideology. Systems of surveillance and censorship aimed at preserving sets of social, political, cultural, philosophical, and religious values exist, in varying degrees of constraint, all over the world. In "Marxist-Leninist" regimes the objective is to ensure that nothing in the country's cultural and intellectual activities will run counter to, or undermine, the ideological orthodoxy as defined from time to time by the political leadership. To this end, the ruling organization employs specialized watchdogs at various levels of the Party and State apparatus which are linked with a nerve center provided by a commission or bureau of the Central Committee. As a rule, the leadership itself will not intervene in these processes, unless it wishes to capitalize on a particularly striking development in the domain in question; most of the time, it will be content with one of its members having over-all responsibility for the whole sector, or for the work of the Central Committee's specialized body.

There is no such laxity in China. Since the Cultural Revolution at least, there is probably not one work of fiction —novel, film, play, opera, or ballet—that has not been scrutinized at Politburo level before its release to the general public or to more or less restricted audiences ("leading cadres," for instance). The quantity of works thus released during the past ten years or so is extremely small, especially in relation to the presumable needs of the Chinese public. As to quality, it does seem that less culturally deprived audiences would have let much of the material involved quickly slip into oblivion. Although the leadership in Peking evinces from time to time a measure of concern at this situation, the room for possible "liberalization" has been and remains strictly limited. Showing once again pre-Cultural Revolution films which had been approved in their time by men now back in power, or calling on the expertise of old artists and writers only too keenly aware of the nature of their mandate (the praise of the socialist regime and of its leaders), hardly amounts to adventurous expeditions into *terra incognita.*

The control directly exercised by the leadership itself is unlikely to be diminished. When the active core of the Politburo sets out to discuss (cf., Teng Hsiao-ping vs. the "Gang of Four") and perhaps heatedly debate a work of art, for what would be seen elsewhere as inordinate amounts of time on the part of extremely busy leaders, they do so for overriding reasons. As in Stalinist regimes, art and literature constitute a permanent "front line," and it is important that the proponents of the politically "correct line" remain dominant and vigilant in the face of never-ceasing attacks by hydra-like heresies. But, because Chinese tradition hardens and sanctifies the classic Marxist approach, in the People's Republic the very existence of art and literature tends to be denied when they are seen not to meet the moral standards set by orthodoxy: today, much as two or three thousand years ago, music is not music if it is deemed to be morally corrupting.[8] On those exalted heights, who else than the supreme rulers themselves will pass judgement on works of art? And so they do, betraying the same predilection as did other occupants of the Dragon's throne for moral and political dissertation, and for poetry of a similarly high order.

At the local level, that is, in the rural areas where 85 percent of the Chinese still live and work, the scene changes. From district level (there are some 2,000 of them in the People's Republic) to work brigade level, the Party Committee secretary enjoys a wide autonomy of decision vis-à-vis higher authority. Like his mandarin predecessors, he is part of a political, ideological, and intellectual elite; Jack of all trades, he is "red and expert," the enlightened amateur. He has the organizational expertise of able bureaucrats under any regime, but also the innate conviction that by virtue of his moral rectitude and of his drive for positive action, he will set an example powerful enough to pull the populace in the right direction. Soil improvement, farm mechanization, rural industries, ideological indoctrination, public education: there is no field of human activity in which he is not expected to provide the driving force which will eventually "move mountains." Experts and managers will be expected to provide the necessary logistical support; the Party Committee secretary, much like the "man of worth" Imperial bureaucrats aspired to be, will retain overall political and moral authority.

The People's Republic cinematographic production amply illustrates this role. "The Golden Road," which depicts rural collectivization, "Spring Sprout," a "radical" sketch of a barefoot doctor of Cultural Revolution vintage, the already cited "Breaking Off," all provide examples of how local cadres are expected to tackle by themselves even the most pressing local issues. Once in possession of general guidance issued by central or provincial authority, they are to use their own judgement and rely on their own "political consciousness," in other words, their political acumen supplemented by judicious quotations from the new Classics (Mao Tse-tung Thought, essentially). Rarely do they refer to their superiors. For one thing, the lack of modern means of communication still constitutes for many of them a formidable obstacle. But even as one witnesses a gradual transformation of the rural decor in Chinese films (better roads, more use of automobiles, easier access to telephones, etc.), the local cadre does not appear markedly more dependent on his superiors' advice (whether or not this is a faithful description of the reality is quite possibly another story). He deals singlehandedly with a given situation, sanction from above coming at the end of the episode in the shape of a letter of approval sent by the Party Chairman ("Breaking Off"), a congratulatory meeting organized by the next higher echelon of the Party ("Spring Sprout"), or the happy discovery, in a *People's Daily* editorial written by Mao Tse-tung himself, that one has followed the "correct line" all along ("The Golden Road").

The perplexed expressions which during a good deal of the action differentiate the heroes of those films from the other characters, reflect—refer to film synopses—the cadres' deep awareness of the complexities of the struggle continuously raging between the "two lines" (the "correct" and the"deviationist" line) within the Party. In other words, one has more or less candidly conveyed to Chinese audiences the uncertainties which frequently, if not permanently, besiege the minds of local Party cadres: what does the "center" actually want? What is really expected of me in the present juncture? How does it fit in with the local situation? How does it affect my own position here?

The Cultural Revolution and the long war of succession which ended in October 1976 have sharply aggravated existing tendencies in the local functionary to see any new problem in terms of a veritable dilemma. So much so, in fact, that during the same decade, central authority has time and again shown its disquiet at this trend, and tried to instill a measure of self-confidence in the minds of its demoralized local servants. But in the best of all Chinas basic contradictions are at all times difficult to solve for state functionaries. Peking tends to speak in edicts whose opacity is due both to reasons of form and to reasons of substance. Expressions of the Center's will are traditionally expected to reflect a profound and unique knowledge of the Classics—be they Confucian or Marxist-Leninist; they are written in a style which puts them in a special category altogether. At the same time, efforts are made, and carefully concealed, to accommodate different currents at or near the top of the hierarchy, and to find a language applicable to a majority of the Chinese people.

But, quite apart from that, the mandate of local representatives of central authority is so wide and so crucial that there cannot but be perpetual conflict in their minds as to the type of relationship which ideally should obtain between them and higher authority.

In this regard, the situation of the committee secretary *mutatis mutandis* is not unsimilar to that of the provincial mandarin in Imperial China. Both have over-all responsibility for the preservation of law and order; both attend to this part of their duties relying in the main on the support of local forces (militia in particular) and notables. The landed and the educated who used to form in Chinese villages an equivalent of erstwhile Western gentries have given way to a new class of "responsible" people: members of the so-called "Revolutionary committees," through which the State extends its apparatus down to the grass roots; members and candidate-members of the Communist Party; members of the mass organizations—women, youth, labor—which relay to the masses where and when necessary the Party's calls for action. Differences between the now defunct "gentry" and its successors are evident: a cultural and social linkage has been broken and its material base destroyed. But because they enjoy diverse forms of access to authority, to better living and to "back-door" (hou men) favoritism and because they provide indispensable and privileged support to the Party cadre, the Chinese gentry's successors have, from the beginnings of the People's Republic, exhibited symptoms of gentrification. That the Chinese Communist Party has all along been aware of this disposition is evinced by its repeated appeals for an austere and altruistic way of life, coupled with promises of spiritual and material advancement for all in the future; witness the publicity surrounding the model agricultural brigade of Tachai, the way its cadres are one with the masses, the fastidious egalitarianism which is seen to pervade all aspects of the life and work of the brigade's members, irrespective of their personal rank and position. One feels urged to exclaim: "See how equal they are!" and proceeds to wonder how far that society has gone toward becoming a replica of the old social pyramid.

Going hand in hand with the preservation of law and order, ideological guidance is another of the important functions assigned essentially to the Confucian as well as to the Marxist functionary in the provinces. Of course, mass media—first and foremost the radio, then newspapers and television—are now entering the countryside in earnest. But the language which prevails in most of the literature thus disseminated, especially in speeches, editorials, and leading doctrinal articles is so stilted and so stereotyped that, whatever degree of literacy has been achieved among the masses, the populace still looks to its cadre for explanation, elucidation, and guidance, as was the case when mandarins received Imperial edicts. The task, exhausting and fraught with perils in times of political crisis, is at best very demanding: from recurring campaigns of "socialist education" aimed at rekindling the revolutionary ardor of the people, to the perpetual search for ideological "correctness" on a doctrinal course which, both in dialectical and in actual terms, is essentially a zig-zag course, the communist cadre's educational duties seem to be endless. But so were, at least theoretically, those of the mandarin, who was expected

to be "father and mother" to the people in his custody.
Here again, and quite expectedly, notables—gentry and
their successors—play a crucial role in support of the
representatives of central authority. The moral pressure
embodied in these representatives finds social and, if need
be, physical assistance in their local allies; the Chinese
version of this far from unique process is remarkable on two
counts: its antiquity and its effectiveness.

Once more in the history of China, this tandem
association is now faced with a formidable challenge.
As always, it is primarily responsible for the welfare of its
corresponding territorial echelon. Central authority, under
the People's Republic, is undoubtedly tempted to extend the
field of its interventions in the ways both industrialized
and developing states do elsewhere; but, out of a mixture of
expediency and traditionally accepted wisdom, it still leaves
much scope—and a large measure of responsibility—to
indigenous initiative and "self-reliance" in practically all
matters. This is strikingly evident in the rhetoric surrounding
the present "four modernizations" program (agriculture,
industry, defence, science and technology), particularly
where it applies to rural zones: districts, communes,
brigades, each under the leadership of their Party committee
must be a decisive factor in the success, or the failure, of
the break-through envisaged by the end of the century.
The objective goes beyond the problem of feeding a huge and
still fast-growing population. It encompasses an impressive
range of options directly bearing on the social fabric of
China: development of rural-based and rural-oriented
industries, gradual reduction of inequalities between town
and country, bringing up a new type of rural worker
combining the expertise of an agriculturist with that of an
industrial technician. There seems to be little reason to doubt
that, once the Center's meager resources in funds,

steel, and high-yield chemical fertilizers are apportioned, and its general guidelines defined, much will depend, once more, on the ingenuity of the modern heirs of the old mandarin-gentry tandem.

Given the magnitude of the tasks central authority expects the bureaucrats to perform, and the freedom of initiative which, *nolens volens*, it allows them, it is hardly surprising that certain constraints should have been developed and maintained under successive Chinese rulers as a counterweight to the growth of potential rivals from seats of local power.

Centralized authoritarian regimes of the kinds China has known ascribe a role in that respect to the masses. Individuals, or groups of them, traditionally have a right to petition the supreme ruler. This practice has provided Emperors and Party Chairmen with opportunities to check on official reports and, more generally, to feel the pulse of the country or at least parts of it. The probability that redress or reform will follow may be remote at best, but activists among Chinese rulers have seen the wisdom of keeping such a channel open. After Mao Tse-tung's death, the Chinese press emphasized that the late Chairman "frequently" read and answered letters coming from the masses; his successor, it was therefore assumed, favored this means of communication, as well as the practice, which newspapers tried to revive from the end of 1976, of writing directly to the editors of the regime's press organs.

The selection of representatives of the masses in China may be equated, today like yesterday, with choosing notables who will be deemed, for a variety of reasons, capable of helping in local government. Whether, as today, a proportion of those people are gathered in national congresses is not immaterial; they certainly do not meet in Peking to share in the exercise of central authority, but it is another way of using their abilities and local standing to push local administration on what are seen at the top level as the right tracks.

The processes of selection have nothing to do with the forms of parliamentary democracy; rather, they entail sometimes lengthy and intricate operations involving power-sharers at all levels of the hierarchy: investigations, discreet opinion polls, definition and negotiation of the internal equilibrium to be preserved. To be sure, this system resembles the Great Wall, in the sense that it is only as good as the people who man it; but it does provide the masses with the hope that, under certain conditions, they will be heard. Chinese films, more often than not, harp on an implicit promise of a related kind: sooner or later the bad among the cadres will be unmasked by the Party with the help of the masses.

This, in fact, is only one aspect of the relationship of mutual control obtaining between Chinese bureaucrats and the populace they administer. Bureaucratic rule has long engulfed the whole of Chinese society in a dense network of criss-cross surveillance to which—once it was basically resurrected after 1949—the Communist regime has only added refinements. In the spring of 1977, for instance, Peking called on the entire industrial sector to follow the example set by the Taching oilfield in Manchuria, from which China derives a large part of its oil. The Taching cadres had adopted a set of regulations ensuring virtually total control, both vertical and horizontal, of everybody's work and life in the field by colleagues, subordinates, and superiors. The systematic stimulation of "shame" reflexes one finds in both Confucian and Chinese communist traditions of moral education probably explains in good part the enduring success of such techniques.

Effective autocrats everywhere tend to be voracious

consumers of reports. Chinese rulers, sitting as they do at the apex of a very sophisticated system of surveillance, have maintained a tradition of personal and intense involvement in its operation. Righteous Emperors rose before dawn to face an endless stream of reports, petitions and advice, annotating those documents which attracted their attention; Mao Tse-tung's and Chou En-lai's bodyguard and personal attendants described, after the two leaders had died, how they would work late at night, sometimes until the small hours of the morning, to keep abreast of all available information on party and state affairs.

According to an article (*People's Daily* of September 8, 1977) signed by the General Office of the Party Central Committee (the organ in charge of inner Party security), Mao in 1955 ordered the 8341 unit (which provides a pretorian guard for Central Committee leaders) to select within its ranks men from each of the country's prefectures, with instructions to return to their native localities, conduct discreet enquiries on the progress of rural collectivization, and report directly and secretly to the Chairman himself. Mao was hardly innovative in this instance: Manchu Emperors used to handpick functionaries at various levels of the mandarin hierarchy to bypass official channels, and obtain parallel and trustworthy information—even if at the cost of painstakingly cross-checking it for themselves. Where Mao Tse-tung possibly improved on past practice was in stipulating that agents of the 8341 unit should include relatives and relations in the field of their intelligence-gathering errands.

There is little reason to think this was an exceptional measure. Various political systems, including the more liberal, have found it desirable to keep open at the same time a variety of knowingly or unknowingly competing channels of confidential information. As to the Chinese

Communist Party, it had certainly tried out formulas of that kind prior to its accession to power in 1949.

The fastidiousness demonstrated by Chinese rulers in their search for reliable information is also reflected in other ways. Mao, like Emperors of the past, put great emphasis on inspection tours in different parts of the country; Hua Kuo-feng is described as faithfully and fruitfully following his example. These tours are not only meant to bring the populace and its ruler in physical contact; they are conceived in terms of on-the-spot, personal investigations, designed, once again, to provide central authority with the means to cross-check official reporting on a given field or region of activity.

Retribution, as far as the bureaucracy is concerned, ultimately lies in the hands of the supreme ruler. Mandarins and cadres alike know that, in the final analysis, it is his privilege to decide what form of legal violence will punish their misdeeds or their felonies. They face, like others, an enduring and impressive set of indigenous recipes of repression combining a high degree of pragmatism with a complete absence of squeamishness.

A recent article by the Public Security Ministry (*People's Daily* of November 28, 1977) is enlightening in this respect. The "theoretical group" (probably the leading group of that department) which signed this text clearly has no qualms about the death penalty: the overriding criterion is that it should never be resorted to when not necessary. This, on the whole, has always been the line of conduct of great Emperors, the same sovereigns who, as a rule, contributed handsomely to the holocausts which punctuate Chinese history. Mao Tse-tung, for his part, deals very frankly and uninhibitedly in the fifth volume of his selected writings with the topic of physical elimination, either massive in the case of the rural "landlord" class, or selective in the case of intellectuals.[9]

Similarly, "labor reform" (i.e., ideological reform through labor camps) is seen as a completely legitimate part of the state's legal arsenal. To the Chinese reader, there may be a cruel irony in the reminder that, in Mao's words, "reform comes first, labor second." To those responsible for carrying out the sentences of the Center, the possibility—faint as it may be—of ultimate redemption is what should matter. Banishment of disgraced mandarins to distant provinces often meant death by illness or at the hands of unruly populations; but it also carried at least the shadow of a promise of rehabilitation if one proved one's worth in those difficult circumstances.

This leads to the other half of the picture. There is also a constant tendency to regard even the most solemn verdicts as essentially transient. Chinese literature of the past abounds with examples, historical and fictional, of mandarins dragged out of prison and disgrace to be reinstated in their former functions or even called to higher ones. The reasons vary: new evidence has been found to throw a different light on their case; a rival has disappeared, suddenly making their particular expertise a desirable commodity, etc. At the very least, this tradition goes some way in explaining the ease with which, all things considered, an impressive proportion of the present leadership in Peking has been disgraced during the Cultural Revolution, only to emerge from the abuse heaped on them back in seats of power a few years later—not to mention the twice re-born Teng Hsio-ping.

3

HIERARCHY, LEGITIMACY, AND ORTHODOXY

It would be a hard task to try and disprove that conformism and ritualism are rife in today's China. Endless mass meetings and demonstrations, *pro forma* participation in repetitive *pro forma* political or ideological debates, mechanical quotations of "Marxist-Leninist" classics, have all taken their toll of popular enthusiasm and spontaneity since the founding of the People's Republic. Listening, for instance, to Peking Radio's "Children's Corner" is an enlightening exercise: kindergarten voices will quite implausibly declaim in sagacious or militant tones how "re-reading attentively" this or that passage of Chairman Mao's writings has brought them a clear realization of how wicked the newly discovered heretic or traitor to the Party had really been through all the years of his or her regrettable career.

Social and political pressures are apparently so pervasive and so effective that few, if any, in China do not go through the required motions. Quite evidently, mechanical conformism prevails most of the time in other Communist states, reflecting a constant and major failure of "Marxist-Leninist" regimes which can also be detected in the People's Republic. But there is arguably something much more atavistic in the Chinese case, in the sense that centuries of Confucian formalism do seem to account at least in part for the remarkable degree of acquiescence shown by the Chinese masses.[10]

Ruling bureaucracies tend to conceive the best of all worlds as a perfect bureaucracy: this trait has perhaps never been more accentuated than in Confucian bureaucracies. They all share the belief that society must be exactingly hierarchic, that it must rest on a universal network of roles which at all times will be precisely defined and correctly filled. In many ways, the People's Republic lives up to the fundamental expectations of all Confucians since Confucius. Consider, for instance, the manner in which it corrects aberrations in its leaders' public behavior. After the disgrace of the "Gang of Four," the new leadership denounced *urbi et orbi* the fact that the Shanghai group had shamelessly manipulated the mass media they controlled in order to alter, through press photographs and television newsreels, popular perceptions of the official order of precedence at the apex of the hierarchy. Not only had they not correctly filled their roles as national leaders, but they had tried to usurp parts they were not supposed to play. There is here an element of moralistic reprobation which Soviet re-writers of history, for instance, can only simulate.

Such an approach to social and political organization does open the way to authoritarian temptations and to a fatalistic acceptance of despotism. At the very least, Chinese bureaucracies have traditionally shown extreme suspicion of potential competition, even from the grassroots (clan or family associations, religious or professional groupings). In fact, ties of personal friendship have long constituted the sole exception to be in turn tolerated or encouraged, as attested by classic novels as well as recent film production (see, among others, the two heroes of "Sea Eagle").

There is, however, a balancing element, or a saving virtue, contained in the notions entertained by and about Chinese bureaucracy. At the core of the problems facing human society, the ruling class's moral worth is seen as what matters more than anything else. Chinese servants of the state are not only expected to be technically able, but also and above all to provide examples of conduct which will set the standards of civilized life. The message may seem to have changed in this century: under Mao Tse-tung and Hua Kuo-feng, Communist cadres at all levels are called upon to "take the lead and set an example" in all imaginable fields of human endeavor, whereas Confucian or neo-Confucian mandarins were concerned with a much more diffuse influence on the masses. But the basic concept remains the same, linking inextricably the exercise of authority and its moral justification.

Leaders and led are not faced with the same demands. The masses are required to follow the examples and directions provided by the "men of worth," or by their modern Communist successors; to guide it, the populace is given vademecums which will impart basic elements of Confucianism, or—today—"Marxism-Leninism." Under the Confucian order there were books for the moral progress of the masses ("Shan shu"); since the establishment of the People's Republic there has been "The Little Red Book," and varying assortments of other texts drawn from Chairman Mao's selected writings. Mandarins and cadres must set their sights higher. The "man of worth," in the neo-Confucian trend predominant under the last Imperial dynasty, was expected to strive continuously through intense philosophical and moral effort, for self-improvement; an exacting scrupulosity was supposed to keep permanent watch on the directions taken by his innermost thoughts. The "good Communist," whether described by the former President of the People's Republic, Liu Shao-chi, or in a wealth of books and films released in the People's Republic (see, for instance, the 1975 film on the beginnings of the Taching oilfield, translated alternatively as "Enterprise" or "The Pioneers"), makes his way on an arduous road, always scrutinizing his own impulses and motivations, endlessly referring to "Marxist-Leninist" classics, permanently aiming at improving his "political consciousness" and his grasp of ideology.

A "man of worth," the servant of the state in his most perfect embodiment, is also a man of letters and a patron of the arts. His moral achievements and intellectual excellence are often reflected in his own mastery of poetry and of its constant companion: calligraphy. This tradition is very much alive today. Echoes of a leader's political and moral worth are found in the quality and elevation of his poems; their publication, along with a facsimile of the original writing, is one of the ultimate forms of public recognition of his merits.

One should not confuse this trait with the poetry everybody is seen to indulge in today in the People's Republic. In the spring of 1977, for example, after Hua Kuo-feng's grand tour of the Taching oilfield, many of the workers who had seen him spent a "sleepless night" composing joyous hymns and poetic pieces. The poetry offered for national consecration belongs to a different order, that of a literature mirroring the virtue of certain leaders. Mao Tse-tung, but also other famous veterans of the Chinese Communist Party—such as Yeh Chien-ying, Chu Teh, Tung Pi-wu, and Chen Yi—some in the most ancient and abstruse poetic styles, others in more modern language, have at one time or another trod that royal path. It is not the mere pastime of a dying generation of revolutionary veterans who happened to be in many ways the product of the old Imperial order. In 1977, many years after the event, the *People's Daily* featured on its frontpage the original

calligraphy of a Chinese transcription written by Hua Kuo-
feng—when still a provincial official in Hunan—of a local
ethnic minority's worksong.

*   *   *

One must pause here to consider the extraordinary
importance of the written word in Chinese political life.
Ideograms do not only have sets of accepted signification.
Because Chinese literature, as indeed other native forms of
intellectual and artistic activity, has always been fascinated
by examples and precedents of the past, including the most
archaic, ideographic expression has acquired very early the
capacity to convey various layers of meaning. To the
illiterate or the semi-literate, this capacity is infinite and
quasi-magic; to the literate, it unfolds like a painted scroll,
revealing its beauties and its mysteries as one advances in
knowledge. An exceptional vehicle for high culture, it has
also become through the centuries an instrument of political
rule.

In recent years, foreign visitors in China have often been
nonplussed to find their hosts intoning with complete
seriousness a quotation from Chairman Mao which to their
unaccustomed minds sounded like a conundrum: "Stock
foodgrains, dig underground shelters, do not practice
hegemony." What on earth could the elliptic triplet mean?

Had they been constantly faced, as had the local
population, with this slogan's written form—on posters and
banners in the streets, on boards and rocks in the fields—
(and had they shared in the various degrees of reading ability
of the Chinese), their reactions would have been quite
different. At an elementary level, they would have perceived
a fundamental call for action and civic virtue: let China ward

off the twin perils of war and hunger; let her not succumb to the vices of her chief enemy. With a sense of Chinese history—a plentiful commodity in China—they would have seen analogies with the concise but vital directives handed down to their people by the first semi-mythical Emperors. In the recourse to the notion of hegemony they would have found references to one of the darkest periods of their ancient past, and a reminder that China's future lies in her soil, in her self-reliance, and in her national unity.

This, quite evidently, is a far cry from the rhetoric the West thinks typical of political speech. Chinese leaders look for concise, thought-provoking, sometimes awe-inspiring formulas; the language thus refined displays its essential values in its ideographic form.

Not that the Chinese ignore eloquence as it is used elsewhere in the world. Indeed, *ex tempore* exhortation was one of the major weapons of the Red Army during two decades of civil war, and today it still plays a part in local administration. But important speeches made by national leaders are really meant to be read, not spoken, if only because so many passages tend to be incomprehensible on account of their literary style; in fact, they are seldom transmitted "live" to the populace. When they are, one would question the wisdom of this departure from normal practice: members of the Communist leadership seem to be indifferent orators—if not downright lamentable like Lin Piao, witness his 1967 speeches from Tien An Men. Good speakers such as Chou En-lai or Teng Hsiao-ping would appear to be exceptions (Mao's talents in this field, like Stalin's, have been assessed in widely divergent manners). In any case, one would look vainly for the sort of verbal eloquence which de Gaulle or Churchill exemplified: the overwhelming onrush of wave after wave of sonorous and striking words and phrases which left audiences shaken, if not moved to action or dedication.

Political speech is not only thought of as primarily a written text; it must also be made available, if only in its most vital passages, in the author's original calligraphy. Modern technology has developed and multiplied the old techniques of facsimile, but one witnesses the same popular reverence, and the same yearning as in the past, for replicas of the rulers' edicts, directives, or mottos in their own calligraphy.

This passion is not esthetically oriented. Some calligraphies are universally acknowledged as having superior beauty, but in most cases, appreciation of a given handwriting will be very much a matter of subjective appreciation. Some will find Mao's strokes powerful but bordering far too often on the anarchic; others will dismiss Hua Kuo-feng's style as extremely ponderous; Japanese experts have decreed that Teng Hsiao-ping's calligraphy was "slightly feminine," and that of the writer and state functionary Kuo Mo-jo "very masculine"—one would have expected quite the opposite of both the granitic Teng and the willowy Kuo.

What the Chinese look for is something quite different: it is the reflection or the incarnation of their leader's personality, as well as a token of their patronage and protection. Hence the incessant requests, during the rulers' visits or audiences, for autographic samples to be used in newspaper mastheads or on the signboards and flags of schools, regiments, factories, etc.

The importance attached to these external signs of power was once more illustrated in the beginning of 1977 when the facade of the monument built in Mao Tse-tung's memory on Tien An Men square appeared in full view: it was adorned on its four sides with huge golden reproductions of the phrase "Chairman Mao's Mausoleum" in his successor's calligraphy. Far more than a symbolic gesture of filial piety, it told all concerned that Hua Kuo-feng had claimed the heritage of China's Great Leader, and that there was no one left to contest that claim.

There is a parallel to draw here between the People's Republic and the Republic of Korea: South Korean leaders like Syngman Rhee and Park Chung-hee whose upbringing had a strong Confucian slant, have used calligraphy as a symbol of power, with much the same popular response one finds in today's China.

*   *   *

Amid the mass of quotations from Marx, Engels, Lenin, and Stalin which now too often clogs the flow of Chinese official eloquence, one finds, from time to time, an authentic native gem. In his August 1977 report on the Party's constitution, Marshal Yeh Chien-ying, the Communist Party's ranking vice-president, used a phrase (*Chih jen shan jen*) which was officially translated as "knowing your subordinates and making good use of them." This piece of advice was offered in the course of a discussion of the Party's cadre policy.

The translation, though accurate, hardly conveyed the particular flavor of the phrase, nor the intellectual context it evoked in Chinese. Literally, Marshal Yeh had said something which could be roughly put as "know [your] men [and] strive to assign [them] correctly." But there was more to it. The choice of words, possibly prompted by the orator's desire, at that point in his speech, for a finely capsulated formula (his poems are famous for their mystifying literary allusions), was fascinating: both "chih" and "shan" are key notions in Chinese traditional thinking,

especially in Confucian discourse. "Shan" carries the notions
of moral amelioration, or advancement. "Chih" refers to a
particular conception of knowledge. One of the cardinal
Confucian virtues, its cultivation was not aimed at
accumulating or increasing ideational concepts or expertise
in diverse fields, intellectual or otherwise; the objective it
embodied was the acquisition of correct moral attitudes.
Training and educating one's mind was one thing; improving
one's moral personality to the point where one would react
correctly in any given situation was another and quite
superior endeavor: the "man of worth" would be concerned
with the latter. Thus, one is brought back to the central
notion that, provided the country has righteous rulers, other
things will fall in place. Yeh Chien-ying had professed in
classical language a belief which is steeped in Chinese
tradition and at the same time very close to the heart of
Maoist thought.

There would be little justification in speculating further on
the use of the expression "Chih jen shan jen." But this
unexpected application of the "make the old serve the new"
Maoist motto does serve a purpose in drawing attention to
the way Chinese intellectual history makes itself felt today
under a regime whose revolutionary credentials are probably
better than most.

Communist regimes all over the world exhibit comparable
symptoms of fundamental conservatism. "Leftist" or
anarchist tendencies are viewed by all of them as the most
dangerous of all aberrations. In the case of the People's
Republic, it is interesting to note that such tendencies
have been recurrent, and that they have found insurmount-
able obstacles in the allied forces of Stalinist conservatism
and traditional Chinese political wisdom.

Political thought in China has long been interested in the
morality of power; in search of it, it has sought inspiration

and guidance primarily in historical precedents. Revolution is very much part of the picture; indeed, it is as old as Imperial unification. But it is seen as a means to regain the Golden Age of a semi-mythical past; each succeeding dynasty in turn claims to have recaptured the ways of the ancients, and concerns itself with consolidating orthodoxy as it sees it. To be sure, the importation of foreign doctrines (Buddhist, Christian, Marxist) has injected important elements of innovation, and brought about a partial rupture with that tradition. But it has not stemmed the native passion for moral justification and historical continuity.

Keeping records of the rulers' actions and writing official history have been from the very beginnings of Imperial China considered an integral part of government. A running commentary of the dynasty's progress was supposed to provide essential guidance to the leaders and to the led, and the dynasty had to appear as carrying out consistently the mandate of Heaven, as well as being in harmony with the teachings of the past.

Long before the Soviet Communists developed their own techniques in rewriting history, Chinese historians had demonstrated both their obsessive concern and their agility in terminological acrobatics aimed at redressing what were denounced as distortions of proper doctrine. Threatening with capital punishment—as in the Book of Rites—those guilty of "confounding names so as to change what has been definitely settled," was in a sense already an admission that it would be an uphill task to keep this evil away from China.

It is worth recalling this background when looking at the political scene in Peking from 1975 to 1977. In the summer of 1975, Teng Hsiao-ping had taken from the failing hands of Chou En-lai the direction of a "normalization" which after "nine years of Cultural Revolution" was to put China back on the course it had followed before the extraordinary upheaval of the late sixties. But, from November of the same year until literally the eve of the "Gang of Four's" disgrace, the Chinese press and radio which was then under the Gang's "fascist dictatorship"—as it came to be described after October 1976—had no more urgent work, except reporting on Chairman Mao's funeral, than to demonstrate that Teng Hsiao-ping was busily, and criminally, "reversing the verdicts" of the Cultural Revolution.

To this end, the arguments put forward by Teng in his 1975 reform plans were refuted one by one *ad libitum*. At the same time, a determined effort was made by press and radio to prove that the man himself as well as his friends had never been trustworthy. This was done quite boldly, through casting aspersions on the achievements of the "seventeen years" which had preceded the Cultural Revolution—in other words those years when, from the founding of the People's Republic, Teng and the "generation of old Revolutionaries" had proved their worth as leaders and administrators of the new regime. Immediately after the downfall of the "Gang of Four," the same media feverishly ridding themselves of all "traces and remnants" of the heretics' influence, seemed to outdo themselves in meticulously retracing their steps. They described how the "Gang of Four," those "pseudo-leftists" who really belonged to the "extreme right" had repeatedly brought the Cultural Revolution to the brink of disaster and civil war. They also refuted one by one the attacks made on Teng's programs, and emphasized the overwhelmingly positive records of the "seventeen years" in question. In 1978, this campaign was obviously far from over.

Amazing as some of the contortions involved in these *volte-faces* may be, there is little profit in simply deriding them: political life under any regime always has its share of antics. What is of interest here is the manner in which first Teng's enemies, then the enemies of Teng's enemies, got to work through the mass media to discredit the opposing faction completely and on all planes: political, ideological, moral, and historical. The effort was tremendous; not one aspect of the enemy's life, work, and personality could be left out, not one mitigating factor left intact. Although very much in the Stalinist tradition, the enterprise was arguably more elaborate and ambitious than the Moscow trials: the destruction of a heretic's political and moral stature must be carried out in such a way as to make it fit as closely as possible, both dialectically and ideologically, in the jigsaw puzzle of the Party's official history.

Other lessons can be drawn from the last stages of the struggle for Mao Tse-tung's succession. One episode is perhaps particularly worth mentioning. Teng Hsiao-ping had been accused by the Shanghai group of having tampered with some of Mao's directives. Quite fittingly, the Shanghai group was officially denounced as having done far worse, namely having used, as a stepping-stone in their conspiracy to seize supreme power, a doctored version of what appeared to be an ultimate adjuration of the dying Chairman to the divided leadership he was leaving behind.

The infamous four had managed to publicize during the first few weeks following Mao's death a phrase which read: "Act according to principles laid down." Hua Kuo-feng, one was later told, waited with characteristic prudence for the implications of the distorted message to dawn on the rest of the leadership (i.e., a veiled injunction to respect the status quo at the top of the hierarchy). When things had suitably matured, he quietly annotated, as Emperors had so often done in the past when dealing with state matters, an official document which happened to quote the "Gang of Four's" version of Mao's posthumous message. The Chairman's "good successor" simply stated that the quotation contained "a couple of faulty characters," but the plotters knew they had lost the battle. When the correct phrase came out— "Follow past practices," a far less cumbersome admonition— they had already been arrested. The gang's "towering crime" is magnificently reminiscent of countless stories of usurpers in the Emperor's closest entourage, who upon their sovereign's death, steal the Imperial seal in a sacrilegious attempt to impose their will on the nation. Whatever its factual bases are, the incident illustrates graphically some of the more constant aspects of Chinese political life.

*   *   *

"Oppose Revisionism" (*Fan Hsiu*)—this battle cry has been much in evidence in the People's Republic, especially since its break with the Soviet Union. It has at times been coupled with another slogan (*Tou szu*) which could be translated as "fight egotism." To some Christian moralists abroad, this last phrase sounded admirable—was it not indicative of a will to shape a truly "new man," an aspiration which had for so long been lacking in institutional Christianity? Did it not dye in quite a different hue the red star over China?

The confusion, though understandable, was prodigious. The egotism (szu) in question referred to everyman's tendencies to self-conceit, selfishness, self-centeredness, and self-indulgence. To "fight egotism" did include a reference to the necessary development of altruistic reflexes of a help-thy-neighbor type, not very far removed in fact from the Christian variety. Communist parties and regimes have constantly emphasized the moral and political value of such reflexes which, in the case of China, happen to have been noticeably absent from the native habitual comportment. A pre-Cultural Revolution film, for instance, underlines, perhaps unconsciously, this latter trait when describing how a policeman in mufti betrays his true identity simply by rushing to help a child who has stumbled and fallen a few feet from him. And yet, commendable as a spirit of "proletarian" brotherhood may be in many respects, it was hardly the prime objective ascribed to "fight egotism" campaigns in China. Indeed, the Party was certainly not concerned with charity here; "egotism" was really first and foremost a pejorative substitute for distinct or discrete opinions—tendencies to see things in a narrow, personal way which, leading one away from the Party's guidance, would inevitably make one more susceptible to revisionist influences.

Christian explorers of today's China (who seem to have forgotten the Inquisition) would perhaps find useful information in Confucian dissertations on the differences between "chih," the kind of moral "knowledge" which keeps one on the path of rectitude, and "szu yi," or "personal opinion " which invariably reflects one's egotistic tendencies: the "man of worth" must bring "knowledge" to dominate "personal opinion," which in essence is incorrect because it is biased by self-interest.

The preoccupation with fighting "szu" (personal=distinct =selfish) tendencies is a reflection of the fundamental notion in Confucianist thought that there are not different conceptions of a given problem. One may hesitate over different methods of tackling it, and wish to be enlightened as to the best way to deal with it; but if one is endowed with the right sort of moral rectitude one will know what lies at the end of the road.

Heroes, either legendary or real, of Chinese Communist lore are no different. They will wonder at times at the ways

and means conducive to the best solution of a given problem
—and usually find the answer in "Mao Tse-tung Thought";
but their outlook on the basic merits of the case will be
correct, and exclude differing opinions on the nature of the
problem. Thus, with both Confucianists and Chinese
Communists, differing opinion tends to be indicative of an
absence of moral, and ideological, rectitude: there is
an affinity of a kind between the Middle Kingdom's
political tradition and Lenin's rationale for his treatment of
dissent within and without the Bolshevik ranks.

Attitudes of this sort cannot but have very definite
practical consequences for the community as well as for the
individual. "Loyal" opposition is unknown to the People's
Republic as much as it was to the Empire. Neither has ever
acknowledged the legitimacy of an opposition which would
be a constituent part of the political system; both have been
content with encouraging from time to time, within narrow
and dangerously fluctuating limits, the expression of what is
called in today's China "constructive criticism," in other
words, carefully self-censored suggestions proffered in an
eminently "positive" frame of mind. Mao's own dynamic
conception of politics has at times led to unique tensions, but
basically nothing has changed. His "scientific thesis" of
the two contending "lines" within the Chinese Communist
Party has certainly done nothing to legitimize dissent in
Chinese political life. In the context of an ongoing and acute
"class struggle," the Party will perforce know a seemingly
endless succession of divisive heresies, which it will
overcome if it keeps a clear awareness of this "law of
history"; the dividing line between right and wrong, tor-
tuous as it may often seem, leaves no room for any conceiv-
able accommodation of a legitimate opposition.

The Great Educator's thesis on the "two lines" has, as far
as the outside world is concerned, at least one merit:

it emphasizes the way opposition in the People's Republic has tended to center on access to power through covert wars of succession. Jockeying for places of influence and patronage, shifting alliances of factions, all within the system and behind the mirrors of ideology, have involved the regime's principal actors in protracted warfare of a basically unlawful and dangerous nature. This again finds multiple echoes in the history of Imperial China.

Individual attitudes—for all practical purposes, a preserve of the ruling bureaucracies—are firmly channeled in the right directions: the Communist functionary, much like his Confucian predecessor, is expected to bring a contribution to public life which, in the ideological perspective of the times, will be "positive" and exemplary. Since political and ideological orthodoxy is consistently commented upon in moral terms, it follows that the political fortunes of a given servant of the state will be deemed to reflect his degree of moral rectitude, or the absence of it. Political disgrace will be assessed along parallel professional and moral standards; political rehabilitation will carry a revision of past verdicts regarding his morals, often at the expense of former accusers, if no more convenient scapegoat can be found. Here again, Stalinist practices of discrediting a political enemy's moral personality have added little to Chinese native usage, while lacking its inherent flexibility: disgrace and rehabilitation have long been two sides of the same coin in Chinese political life.

The masses, in this process, play the part of the antique Greek chorus. Their eyes have always been "sharp" and everywhere—a tradition which arguably has made it comparatively easy for the Communists to institutionalize and render more sophisticated past patterns of collective and mutual surveillance. Courtyards' committees may poetically be "turned toward the Sun" (*Hsiang Yang Yuan*) (in other words toward the "Marxist-Leninist" sun whose abode is Peking); nothing much escapes their permanent watchfulness. Gifted with a long memory, the masses will remain staunchly silent for as long as their cadres will be seen to enjoy the confidence of higher authority. But when it is gone, they will be ready to provide overwhelming, and if need be damning, evidence of practically everybody's foibles or outright depravity. The Cultural Revolution has, of course, furnished numerous instructive examples of this disposition; but outside of this unique situation, the campaign of "criticism" of the "Gang of Four," for instance, has also produced a wealth of testimonies which, contrived as they may appear to be in many respects, do seem to contain at least a modicum of factual evidence on the private life of those former "leaders of the Party and Nation."

*   *   *

To try to speak of intellectuals in China in the way one discusses the social and political role of the intelligentsia elsewhere in the world is perhaps irrelevant and certainly misleading. Mandarins were not only in charge of the reigning orthodoxy's defense and propagation, they were also essentially men of letters. Their access to the Imperial bureaucracy depended on literary excellence, to which they often added virtuosity in other artistic disciplines: calligraphy, painting, music. In a very literal sense, therefore, the Chinese intelligentsia ruled the country. Consider the poets of the Tang Dynasty (the Golden Age of Chinese poetry): many of the very best were state functionaries, some of high hierarchic rank. The equation between high culture and political power was in fact so thorough and so evident that anybody with some literary merit was expected to aspire to a bureaucratic career (see, *inter alia*, the Ching Dynasty novel "Hung lou meng"[11]); as late as in this century when the old Imperial order had finally vanished, students of the first state-run universities saw themselves as part of officialdom.

Individuals, rather than a section or sections of society, stood out on the margin of the ruling intelligentsia: philosophers, political thinkers, poets who had declined or failed to join the ranks of the bureaucracy. They certainly did not live in the most comfortable of all Chinas. Indeed, they were cast, with some justification, in the role of potential, if not practicing, recusants of the social order of their time. But they were also seen in phases of political chaos and dynastic decadence as necessary ferments of change, as providers of new ideas, as purifiers of the old orthodoxy.

In the 1920s, the cultural renaissance which shook the intelligentsia, who by then had been dispossessed of its traditional role, seemed to herald for Chinese intellectuals a new era of deep and prolonged involvement in political affairs. At its beginnings, the Chinese Communist Party, as other political groupings, filled the ranks of its leadership by drawing heavily on precisely those social classes with privileged access to high culture which had traditionally provided the country with its political cadre. At the same time an explosion of journalistic activity spawning hundreds of periodicals representing a wide variety of political persuasions appeared to testify to a profound qualitative change in the life and role of China's intelligentsia, which would ultimately bring it in line with less exotic models abroad.

As these perspectives were taking shape, so were perils directly menacing the emergence of this new section of Chinese society: the rigors of three decades of civil war, Kuomintang censorship, and finally the policy adopted by

the Communists in 1942 at Yenan killed the phoenix before it
could rise. Mao's "talks at Yenan" spelled out with great
clarity the future reserved to "fighters of the literary and
artistic front" under the new regime to come: insofar as they
would survive as a distinct entity, it would be in order to
provide the "new China," in other words "socialism" and
its leaders, with cohorts of hagiographers and coryphaei.
Officially a part of the new bureaucratic order so long
as they accepted its drastic conditions and were in its pay,
writers and artists more often than not remained in fact
on the margin of it: after all, did they not cling suspiciously
to the high culture of the past? Had they not retained a
noxious propensity to act spontaneously as spokesmen for
various forms of dissent?

Under the People's Republic, survivors of this harrowing
journey twice believed they were being called upon to play a
much more active part in political life. During the Hundred
Flowers period in the late fifties and during the beginnings
of the Cultural Revolution (1966-67), more than one felt that
he had a new mandate to challenge the weaknesses and vices
exhibited by the new regime. The intellectuals twice ended
as expendable battalions in the private *Kriegspiel* of the
Communist leadership. Frightened and embittered,
despairing of ever being allowed to produce works meeting
their own standards, they finally pulled out of the game.
The dogmatic and desiccating rule exercised by Chiang
Ch'ing and consorts since the Cultural Revolution over all
forms of art and literature could only harden their resolve to
abstain from any form not only of involvement but of
production. Since the fall of the "Gang of Four" their silence
has hardly been broken except by faint signs of life.

Twice bitten in the past, they look today as if they were scrutinizing rather mirthlessly the leadership's promises of a "new cultural spring" whose most obvious references still seem to be the famous "Yenan talks."

Since the founding of the People's Republic, the question has been asked countless times: could not the cultural and political renaissance as expressed, for instance, in the May 1919 student movement have had a different denouement? A variety of possibilities can of course be explored in answer to that question; but one may legitimately suspect that the more plausible scenarios could be summarized in the answer that yes, it could have had a different ending, but probably not a very different one.

With the Communists in a position of dominance, and given the inherent constraints they brought to political life as a Leninist organization with stigmas of strong Stalinist influence, one envisages various patterns of more or less sophisticated "Marxist-Leninist" rule as it is known elsewhere, combined in varying degrees with native traditions of social and political organization. Without the Communists (for it is doubtful that they would have ever accepted, and been accepted in, the role of a "loyal" opposition) the chaos and devastation wrought by decades of civil war and foreign invasion would have paved the way for the restoration of at least some form of "enlightened despotism" through which a "new China" would have reorganized and re-unified itself under a strong central government.

Speculation of this kind can perhaps be endowed with more substance by looking at political regimes on the fringes of China's traditional zone of cultural influence, especially where it may be assumed that Confucian thought still plays a part in shaping local political thought and attitudes. If one leaves Japan aside, since it has long absorbed successive layers of Chinese influence into its own intellectual processes, one will be tempted to turn first to the "other China," in other words, to Taiwan.

One will soon realize, however, that it cannot offer anything relevant to the question asked. For all practical purposes, the Taiwanese have, since the defeat of Japan in 1945, traded one form of colonial rule for another which combines aspects of colonization by settlement and by administration: the islanders have had to make room for close to two million "mainlanders" and to let them enjoy a quasi-total monopoly on all organs of political and military power. It is extremely doubtful that they have ever perceived the Kuomintang rule as completely legitimate. To be sure, Chiang Kai-shek persevered to the end, on the island as he had on the "mainland," in his efforts to present himself as the one and only legitimate pivot of Chinese national life, in which Taiwan is presumed to share unreservedly as a full-fledged Chinese province. The Generalissimo may not have failed there as conspicuously as on the "mainland" (see *inter alia*, the "Stilwell Papers"); but one is probably not far from popular perceptions if one describes him as a chieftain who fought battles in the cause of a defeated and vanished dynasty, which only concern the island's population because he had turned it into his last bastion.

The measure of his failure would possibly be reflected *a contrario* by Taiwanese popular perceptions of Mao Tsetung as having attained, in so far as China itself is concerned, the very position which always escaped Chiang Kai-shek. The harping on Confucian tradition and values by the Taiwan Kuomintang regime—in particular, at the time of the Cultural Revolution and of the "criticize Confucius" campaign in the People's Republic—has been of no avail. Because it found so few echoes in popular sentiment, and scarcely more in the ruling elite, it has never been much more than a simulated revival sometimes bordering on the farcical. The contrary would indeed have been surprising: after half a century of Japanese colonization, decades of Nationalist imperium, and constant exposure to the onslaught of extreme and conflicting brands of alien propaganda, the native Taiwanese today are bound to be confused and uncertain in their basic loyalties.

But if one turns to what is sometimes called, perhaps not so improperly, a "third China," that is Singapore, one gets possibly nearer to the heart of the problem. Here one has a city-state ruled by one man, Lee Kwan-yew, by means of as disciplined and efficient a bureaucracy as the area has ever known. His power base rests on a political party which has virtually eliminated all rival organizations and all forms of opposition, as well as on a popular consensus of sorts, as elicited from time to time by various means.

To many outside the small republic, its regime has unmistakably authoritarian undertones; to some, it is quite simply a police state. The Socialist International which had welcomed Lee's party quite naturally since it had fought "imperialism" and spoke in Fabian-like terms, recently discovered that it had nursed a viper in its bosom, and was only too relieved to see it withdraw before the organization had to go through the motions of formal expulsion.

Those who saw Lee Kwan-yew as a "tough city boss," or worse, as a Tong chief, overlooked the rationale proffered by a man who, under the brilliant veneer he had acquired in his commerce with Western social democrats, presented many of the traits of a Chinese autocrat. Whatever the depth of his intimate convictions, there is a traditional coherence in the beliefs Lee professes, privately or publicly, as to himself (a kind of modern sage-king providing wise and appropriate guidance to his people, who in turn see him readily in those terms), and as to the morality of power (opposition or militant dissent are not only politically dangerous, but morally wrong; morality in public and private mores must be emphasized). What is also apparent, but also tends to be overlooked, is the fact that the overwhelmingly Chinese population of Singapore maintains, by and large, a not so tenuous link with traditional Confucian concepts of statesmanship and of the relationship between the ruler and the masses.

Another instructive case is that of Korea, which across the centuries has known hierarchized societies closely inspired by, and patterned on, Chinese Confucian models. Under Japanese colonization, and later under the Republic in South Korea, it has gone through a series of neo-Confucian revivals, the last being marked by the adoption of the "Revitalization" Constitution of 1972. The authoritarian inclinations of the chief artisan of these revivals cannot be doubted; nor can the fact that Park Chung-hee, like many of his generation, is deeply imbued, both because of his Korean upbringing and his Japanese education, with traditional Chinese political concepts.

Mutatis mutandis, a parallel could be drawn between "Republican" China's ceaseless torments and some at least of the tensions which, from the inception of the Republic in South Korea, have periodically convulsed it. One may wonder whether there is not something irreconcilable in the dichotomy which seems to afflict societies still adhering in one way or another to Confucian concepts of public life, while at the same time opening themselves up to various gospels of political pluralism.

4

CHINA FOREVER?

On 31 December 1977, the *People's Daily*'s front page attained a pinnacle of exoticism which would surely have delighted Victor Segalen.[12] In lieu of the stolid stocktaking one expects under any regime at that time of the year, the mouthpiece of the Chinese Communist Party Central Committee devoted the entire first page of its daily six pages to poetic dissertation.

The text was provided by the Great Helmsman himself. Mao had written a letter in July 1965 to Marshal Chen Yi, a Party veteran, and it was this particular missive the *People's Daily* now found important enough to publicize in both facsimile and printed transcription.

Did it have any bearing on the struggle between the "two lines," or on the mechanization of agriculture, or the efforts aimed at a new "great leap forward"? Not in the least. Chen Yi ("a bad mayor [of Shanghai] and a worse poet," *dixit* Chang Chun-chiao of the "Gang of Four") had tried his hand at pentameters and submitted a sample of his work to the Chairman, begging for guidance and correction. This, Mao replied, was out of the question. His own efforts, for what they had been worth, had been limited to heptameters. Why not ask instead "Chien-ying" (Marshal Yeh Chien-ying) or better still, "Old Tung" (Tung Pi-wu), who had practiced pentameters?

The letter, however, does not end there. In 1965, Mao Tse-tung had been composing poems on classic models for at least four decades: how could he resist Chen Yi's entreaties? As a matter of fact, he had amended, if ever so triflingly, his old companion's poem, and in the second part of his letter found himself offering erudite advice on where to look in Chinese literature for the right sort of models: Sung and Tang masters, he suggested, had possibly all the answers.

As was often the case, a Mao quotation printed in bold letters in the paper's masthead placed the letter in its true political context. "Let a hundred flowers bloom": once more the country's intellectual elites, and especially "literary and artistic workers," were being urged to rally wholeheartedly to the cause of "socialism." A few days later, the *People's Daily* was to remind all concerned that new prospects had opened for Chinese culture with the coming to power of Mao's "good successor." Armed with Mao Tse-tung's shining directives, writers and artists could now look forward with full confidence to the "new spring" promised by Hua Kuo-feng.

The publication of Mao's twelve-year-old letter illustrates the often bold and imaginative use the new leadership makes of the Great Educator's writings. Far more efficiently than a long-winded, prudently balanced doctrinal article, this document establishes that parts at least of China's traditional high culture are valid and permissible. Because Mao professes quite unrestrainedly his admiration for, and familiarity with, classic poetry, because no less than four of People's China historic leaders are seen to share similar tastes for classical literature, it appears as if suddenly a major bridge leading to China's cultural heritage had again been declared safe and open to the public.

Important as this new gesture may look in the eyes of Chinese intelligentsia, it perhaps deserves to be examined from different and wider angles. The masters of the People's Republic have shown time and again that they are not unaware of the sterility which has gradually but inexorably afflicted most cultural activities under the new regime. If one goes by the care they have taken since Hua acceded to supreme power to present their cultural policy in the most seductive fashion, they know precisely where the heart of the problem lies. Without reneging on the dogma (the Yenan talks), they have earnestly tried to paint in newer and brighter colors the part to be played by writers and artists in "socialist" China.

But something else also seems to emerge at times from the literature devoted by official organs to cultural matters: a new concern for a variety of forms of artistic expression which have played a decisive role in making Chinese civilization both unique and remarkably coherent in its richness. Some will argue that it is far too late in the day to try and search out the last exponents (musical composers and instrumentalists, stage actors and opera singers, artisans in various crafts), of arts which do not belong to the era of highly developed technology the "new China" is supposed to have recently entered in earnest. Others, who now seem to have managed to be heard and listened to by the new leadership, are attempting to revive and popularize those elements of traditional popular and high Chinese culture which may still be preserved or restored. An indirect proof of the authority they enjoy is perhaps to be found in the absence of critical comments from Peking's usual spokesmen in Hong Kong in the face of local efforts aimed at reviving traditional Canton and Chiuchow operas; in other times, one would have expected at least dark mutterings about obscurantist "conspiracies."

Chinese culture is possibly nearing a point of no return; at any rate, decisions taken today concerning the cultural domain will be crucial. Much, if not everything which is really vital, will depend on the preservation of a strong ideographic link with the past. Hope, in that respect, seems justified: mass alphabetization only seems to have exacerbated the native passion for that endless voyage of discovery which "learning to read" Chinese ideograms really is. Look at the rurals crowding into former Imperial palaces and gardens: they will stop in groups in front of archaic bronzes or ancient scrolls, helping one another, as best they can, to stumble through those mystifying but fascinating inscriptions; they will go from one place to another devotedly jotting down in notebooks the most poetic or the most unusual of the characters they discover.

Poetry could play an all-important role in this process. "Spoken" poetic genres exist, and have been favored by the regime for obvious reasons; Marshal Chen Yi, for one, was better known for his poems in "clear [or spoken] language" (pai hua). But the literary language (wen yen) exercises on all poets a most powerful attraction: the generation is possibly not yet born which will not succumb to the infinite charm and sophistication of poets of Tang vintage, and which will not try in its turn to emulate them. Through poetry, and one would suspect, only through it, the Chinese high culture of the past can survive not as the preserve of a rarefied literary elite, but as a truly national domain open, as a birthright, to all Chinese.

Outstanding sinologists will quite convincingly demonstrate that the necessary links with native intellectual tradition have been irretrievably destroyed; that the few remaining representatives of this tradition have no successors; that we have unknowingly witnessed the death pangs of Chinese civilization. One is not bound to share their views. Much as elsewhere, revolutionary change and innovation in China have proved to be compressible; with the passing of time, pride and a passionate interest in China's past have again forcefully emerged not only as facts of civilization, but as elements in the political equation. To be sure, Chinese society has been altered radically. But it does not mean that, in the process, what created the profound originality and richness of Chinese civilization has perforce been bodily jettisoned. To add but two examples to those already cited—the hermetic literature published in the course of the campaign to "criticize Confucius," and the doctrinal articles signed by Yao Wen-yuan of the "Gang of Four," do seem to establish beyond doubt that the Chinese Communist Party's *sanctum sanctorum* itself shelters for better or for worse able and active intellectuals who could legitimately claim to be the heirs of the literati of the past.

5

ONE LAST WORD

Hua fei hua
Wu fei wu

Flower: but is it a flower?
Mist: but is this mist?

Po Chü-yi
772-846

Is this all of any concern to the non-Chinese world? The answer would appear to be that it is indeed of great importance to us.

If one accepts the premise that in spite of Imperial decadence and revolutionary change, China still maintains today important parts of the oldest intellectual and cultural tradition, it is undoubtedly vital to get to know it better in every sense of the word. Civilizations have proved to be dismally short-lived and transient. Some, which we suspect to have achieved unequalled levels of sophistication in certain domains, have vanished leaving behind them the most meager and frustrating clues as to the true nature of the spiritual and intellectual enterprise they briefly embodied. Maya hieroglyphs, for instance, are not just an indecipherable riddle: they are—and this is far more important—a reminder that forms of human knowledge, such as those tentatively attributed by educated guesswork to the Maya, can be lost probably forever.

Also, when reflecting on our short and long-term future, one might do worse than take a close look at the social, political, and intellectual history of the Chinese people. "Revolution cannot be exported," as their Communist leaders have often said, and one will indeed question not only the desirability, but the possibility of duplicating outside of China some of her recent authoritarian experiments in agricultural, industrial, or urban organization. What one could try better to understand, in the face of new and disconcerting problems, is what has enabled this vast and compact conglomerate of men to preserve human relationships which on balance appear to be characterized by a modicum of measure and culture.

1. See Bibliography.

2. See Bibliography.

3. In which the verb in the third person singular emphasizes the collectiveness of a subject in the plural form; literally: "The animals runs."

4. This is not to say that the soldier-citizen ideal was entirely foreign to Mao Tse-tung; nor that the People's Liberation Army, during the civil war, has not produced in great numbers its own brand of soldier-citizen. The point is that even this indigenous type did not survive the establishment of the new regime in 1949. Conversely, one could point out that the "soldat de l'An II" was a very short-lived phenomenon. However, that particular model undeniably left a deep imprint in the collective conscience of the European peoples, and had an important role in the shaping of European nationalisms in the 19th century.

5. There were of course constant tensions and conflicts within the bureaucracy: contending cliques, competing local interests provided for lively, and sometimes destructive, bureaucratic politics.

6. Roxane Witke, *Comrade Chiang Ch'ing: Mao's Wife Self-Revealed* (Boston: Little, Brown, Inc.), 1977.

7. See Bibliography.

8. What was probably unparalleled at any time in Imperial China is the present degree of control exercised by the Communist regime. In the past, heterodox streams of native thought constantly survived, if only in the shape of secret rivulets. Today, controls throughout Chinese society seem to be so pervasive that one may wonder whether this tradition somehow still endures, carrying with it promises of a perhaps distant, but authentic, blossoming of Chinese culture.

9. See Bibliography.

10. "Conformist" as they are, the Chinese people are not sheep- or "ant" -like, as has been amply demonstrated both in the past, by a long history of popular uprisings, and under the present regime, by widespread passive resistance during the Great Leap Forward, or by the Tien An Men "incident" in 1976.

11. See Bibliography.

12. See Bibliography.

BIBLIOGRAPHY

This list of books is merely intended to provide references for the authors and works mentioned in this book. A few titles have been added because they throw an interesting light on the issues discussed here.

François Cheng, *L'écriture poétique chinoise*, Paris, Editions du Seuil, 1977.

Maurice Collis, *Foreign Mud*, New York, Knopf, 1947.

Pierre Gourou, *Man and Land in the Far East*, New York, Longman, 1975.

Emile Guikovaty, *Mao, images d'une vie*, Paris, Laffont, 1976.

Jacques Guillermaz, *The Chinese Communist Party in Power—1949-1976*, Boulder, Westview Press, 1976.

Simon Leys, *Les habits neufs du Président Mao, Ombres chinoises, Images brisées*, Paris, Bibliotheque Asiatique, 1977.

Mao Tse-tung, *Selected Writings* (Volume 5), Peking, 1977. *Poems*, Peking, 1977.

Jean Pasqualini, *Prisoner of Mao*, New York, Penguin, 1973.

Victor Segalen, *Fils du Ciel, René Leys, Lettres de Chine*, Paris, Plon, 1967.

Shen Fu, *Chapters From a Floating Life*, London, Oxford University Press, 1961.

Edgar Snow, *Red Star Over China*, New York, Random House, 1938.

Jonathan D. Spence, *Emperor of China*, New York, Knopf, 1974.

Joseph W. Stilwell, *The Stilwell Papers*, New York, Schocken, 1972.

Tsao Hsue-hsin, *Hung Lou Meng* ("The Story of the Stone"), Harmondsworth, Penguin, 1976-77.

Nym Wales, *Red Dust*, Stanford, Stanford University Press, 1952.

BOOKS WRITTEN UNDER CENTER AUSPICES

The Soviet Bloc, Zbigniew K. Brzezinski (sponsored jointly with the Russian Research Center), 1960. Harvard University Press. Revised edition. 1967.

The Necessity for Choice, by Henry A. Kissinger, 1961. Harper & Bros.

Rift and Revolt in Hungary, by Ferenc A. Váli, 1961. Harvard University Press.

Strategy and Arms Control, by Thomas C. Schelling and Morton H. Halperin, 1961. Twentieth Century Fund.

United States Manufacturing Investment in Brazil, by Lincoln Gordon and Engelbert L. Grommers, 1962. Harvard Business School.

The Economy of Cyprus, by A.J. Meyer, with Simos Vassiliou (sponsored jointly with the Center for Middle Eastern Studies), 1962. Harvard University Press.

Enterpreneurs of Lebanon, by Yusif A. Sayigh (sponsored jointly with the Center for Middle Eastern Studies), 1962. Harvard University Press.

Communist China 1955-1959: Policy Documents with Analysis, with a foreword by Robert R. Bowie and John K. Fairbank (sponsored jointly with the East Asian Research Center), 1962. Harvard University Press.

Somali Nationalism, by Saadia Touval, 1963, Harvard University Press.

The Dilemma of Mexico's Development, by Raymond Vernon, 1963. Harvard University Press.

Limited War in the Nuclear Age, by Morton H. Halperin, 1963. John Wiley & Sons.

In Search of France, by Stanley Hoffman *et al.,* 1963. Harvard University Press.

The Arms Debate, by Robert A. Levine, 1963. Harvard University Press.

Africans on the Land, by Montague Yudelman, 1964. Harvard University Press.

Counterinsurgency Warfare, by David Galula, 1964. Frederick A. Praeger, Inc.

People and Policy in the Middle East, by Max Weston Thornburg, 1964. W.W. Norton & Co.

Shaping the Future, by Robert R. Bowie, 1964. Columbia University Press.

Foreign Aid and Foreign Policy, by Edward S. Mason (sponsored jointly with the Council on Foreign Relations), 1964. Harper & Row.

How Nations Negotiate, by Fred Charles Iklé, 1964. Harper & Row.

Public Policy and Private Enterprise in Mexico, edited by Raymond Vernon, 1964. Harvard University Press.

China and the Bomb, by Morton H. Halperin (sponsored jointly with the East Asian Research Center), 1965. Frederick A. Praeger, Inc.

Democracy in Germany, by Fritz Erler (Jodidi Lectures), 1965. Harvard University Press.

The Troubled Partnership, by Henry A. Kissinger (sponsored jointly with the Council on Foreign Relations), 1965. McGraw-Hill Book Co.

The Rise of Nationalism in Central Africa, by Robert I. Rotberg, 1965. Harvard University Press.

Pan-Africanism and East African Integration, by Joseph S. Nye, Jr., 1965. Harvard University Press.
Communist China and Arms Control, by Morton H. Halperin and Dwight H. Perkins (sponsored jointly with the East Asian Research Center), 1965. Frederick A. Praeger, Inc.
Problems of National Strategy, ed. Henry Kissinger, 1965. Frederick A. Praeger, Inc.
Deterrence before Hiroshima: The Airpower Background of Modern Strategy, by George H. Quester, 1966. John Wiley & Sons.
Containing the Arms Race, by Jeremy J. Stone, 1966. M.I.T. Press
Germany and the Atlantic Alliance:The Interaction of Strategy and Politics, by James L. Richardson, 1966. Harvard University Press.
Arms and Influence, by Thomas C. Schelling, 1966. Yale University Press.
Political Change in a West African State, by Martin Kilson, 1966. Harvard University Press.
Planning Without Facts: Lessons in Resource Allocation from Nigeria's Development, by Wolfgang F. Stolper, 1966. Harvard University Press.
Export Instability and Economic Development, by Alasdair I. MacBean, 1966. Harvard University Press.
Foreign Policy and Democratic Politics, by Kenneth N. Waltz (sponsored jointly with the Institute of War and Peace Studies, Columbia University), 1967. Little, Brown & Co.
Contemporary Military Strategy, by Morton H. Halperin, 1967. Little, Brown & Co.
Sino-Soviet Relations and Arms Control, ed. Morton H. Halperin (sponsored jointly with the East Asian Research Center), 1967. M.I.T. Press.
Africa and United States Policy, by Rupert Emerson, 1967. Prentice-Hall.
Elites in Latin America, edited by Seymour M. Lipset and Aldo Solari, 1967. Oxford University Press.
Europe's Postwar Growth, by Charles P. Kindleberger, 1967. Harvard University Press.
The Rise and Decline of the Cold War, by Paul Seabury, 1967. Basic Books.
Student Politics, ed. S.M. Lipset, 1967. Basic Books.
Pakistan's Development: Social Goals and Private Incentives, by Gustav F. Papenek, 1967. Harvard University Press.
Strike a Blow and Die: A Narrative of Race Relations in Colonial Africa, by George Simeon Mwase, ed. Robert I. Rotberg, 1967. Harvard University Press.
Party Systems and Voter Alignments, edited by Seymour M. Lipset and Stein Rokkan, 1967. Free Press.
Agrarian Socialism, by Seymour M. Lipset, revised edition, 1968. Doubleday Anchor.

Aid, Influence and Foreign Policy, by Joan M. Nelson, 1968. The Macmillan Company.

Development Policy: Theory and Practice, edited by Gustav F. Papanek, 1968. Harvard University Press.

International Regionalism, by Joseph S. Nye, 1968. Little, Brown & Co.

Revolution and Counterrevolution, by Seymour M. Lipset, 1968. Basic Books.

Political Order in Changing Societies, by Samuel P. Huntington, 1968. Yale University Press.

The TFX Decision: McNamara and the Military, by Robert J. Art, 1968. Little, Brown & Co.

Korea: The Politics of the Vortex, by Gregory Henderson, 1968. Harvard University Press.

Political Development in Latin America, by Martin Needler, 1968. Random House.

The Precarious Republic, by Michael Hudson, 1968. Random House.

The Brazilian Capital Goods Industry, 1929-1964 (sponsored jointly with the Center for Studies in Education and Development), by Nathaniel H. Leff, 1968. Harvard University Press.

Economic Policy-Making and Development in Brazil, 1947-1964, by Nathaniel H. Leff, 1968. John Wiley & Sons.

Turmoil and Transition: Higher Education and Student Politics in India, edited by Philip G. Altbach, 1968. Lalvani Publishing House (Bombay).

German Foreign Policy in Transition, by Karl Kaiser, 1968. Oxford University Press.

Protest and Power in Black Africa, edited by Robert I. Rotberg, 1969. Oxford University Press.

Peace in Europe, by Karl E. Birnbaum, 1969. Oxford University Press.

The Process of Modernization: An Annotated Bibliography on the Socio-cultural Aspects of Development, by John Brode, 1969. Harvard University Press.

Students in Revolt, edited by Seymour M. Lipset and Philip G. Altbach, 1969. Houghton Mifflin.

Agricultural Development in India's Districts: The Intensive Agricultural Districts Programme, by Dorris D. Brown, 1970. Harvard University Press.

Authoritarian Politics in Modern Society: The Dynamics of Established One-Party Systems, edited by Samuel P. Huntington and Clement H. Moore, 1970. Basic Books.

Nuclear Diplomacy, by George H. Quester, 1970. Dunellen.

The Logic of Images in International Relations, by Robert Jervis, 1970. Princeton University Press.

Europe's Would-Be Polity, by Leon Lindberg and Stuart A. Scheingold, 1970. Prentice-Hall.

Taxation and Development: Lessons from Colombian Experience, by Richard M. Bird, 1970. Harvard University Press.

Lord and Peasant in Peru: A Paradigm of Political and Social Change, by F. LaMond Tullis, 1970. Harvard University Press.
The Kennedy Round in American Trade Policy: The Twilight of the GATT? by John W. Evans, 1971. Harvard University Press.
Korean Development: The Interplay of Politics and Economics, by David C. Cole and Princeton N. Lyman, 1971. Harvard University Press.
Development Policy II—The Pakistan Experience, edited by Walter P. Falcon and Gustav F. Papanek, 1971. Harvard University Press.
Higher Education in a Transitional Society, by Philip G. Altbach, 1971. Sindhu Publications (Bombay).
Studies in Development Planning, edited by Hollis B. Chenery, 1971. Harvard University Press.
Passion and Politics, by Seymour M. Lipset with Gerald Schaflander, 1971. Little, Brown & Co.
Political Mobilization of the Venezuelan Peasant, by John D. Powell, 1971. Harvard University Press.
Higher Education in India, edited by Amrik Singh and Philip Altbach, 1971. Oxford University Press (Delhi).
The Myth of the Guerrilla, by J. Bowyer Bell, 1971. Blond (London) and Knopf (New York).
International Norms and War between States: Three Studies in International Politics, by Kjell Goldmann, 1971. Published jointly by Läromedelsförlagen (Sweden) and the Swedish Institute of International Affairs.
Peace in Parts: Integration and Conflict in Regional Organization, by Joseph S. Nye, Jr. 1971. Little, Brown & Co.
Sovereignty at Bay: The Multinational Spread of U.S. Enterprise, by Raymond Vernon, 1971. Basic Books.
Defense Strategy for the Seventies (revision of Contemporary Military Strategy) by Morton H. Halperin, 1971. Little, Brown & Co.
Peasants Against Politics: Rural Organization in Brittany, 1911-1967, by Suzanne Berger, 1972. Harvard University Press.
Transnational Relations and World Politics, edited by Robert O. Keohane and Joseph S. Nye, Jr., 1972. Harvard University Press.
Latin American University Students: A Six-Nation Study, by Arthur Liebman, Kenneth N. Walker, and Myron Glazer, 1972. Harvard University Press.
The Politics of Land Reform in Chile, 1950-1970: Public Policy, Political Institutions and Social Change, by Robert R. Kaufman, 1972. Harvard University Press.
The Boundary Politics of Independent Africa, by Saadia Touval, 1972. Harvard University Press.
The Politics of Nonviolent Action, by Gene E. Sharp, 1973. Porter Sargent.
System 37 Viggen: Arms, Technology, and the Domestication of Glory, by Ingemar Dörfer, 1973. Universitets forlaget (Oslo).

University Students and African Politics, by William John Hanna, 1974. Africana Publishing Company.

Organizing the Transnational: The Experience with Transnational Enterprise in Advanced Technology, by M.S. Hochmuth, 1974. Sijthoff (Leiden).

Becoming Modern, by Alex Inkeles and David H. Smith, 1974. Harvard University Press.

The United States and West Germany 1945-1973: A Study in Alliance Politics, by Roger Morgan (sponsored jointly with the Royal Institute of International Affairs), 1974. Oxford University Press.

Multinational Corporations and the Politics of Dependence: Copper in Chile, 1945-1973, by Theodore Moran, 1974. Princeton University Press.

The Andean Group: A Case Study in Economic Integration Among Developing Countries, by David Morawetz, 1974. M.I.T. Press.

Kenya: The Politics of Participation and Control, by Henry Bienen, 1974. Princeton University Press.

Land Reform and Politics: A Comparative Analysis, by Hung-chao Tai, 1974. University of California Press.

Big Business and the State: Changing Relations in Western Europe, edited by Raymond Vernon, 1974. Harvard University Press.

Economic Policymaking in a Conflict Society: The Argentine Case, by Richard D. Mallon and Juan V. Sourrouille, 1975. Harvard University Press.

New States in the Modern World, edited by Martin Kilson, 1975. Harvard University Press.

Revolutionary Civil War: The Elements of Victory and Defeat, by David Wilkinson, 1975. Page-Ficklin Publication.

Politics and the Migrant Poor in Mexico City, by Wayne A. Cornelius, 1975. Stanford University Press.

East Africa and the Orient: Cultural Syntheses in Pre-Colonial Times, ed. H. Neville Chittick and Robert I. Rotberg, 1975. Africana Publishing Company.

No Easy Choice: Political Participation in Developing Countries, by Samuel P. Huntington and Joan M. Nelson, 1976. Harvard University Press.

The Politics of International Monetary Reform—The Exchange Crisis, by Michael J. Brenner, 1976. Ballinger Publishing Co.

The International Politics of Natural Resources, by Zuhayr Mikdashi, 1976. Cornell University Press.

The Oil Crisis, edited by Raymond Vernon, 1976. W.W. Norton & Co.

Social Change and Political Participation in Turkey, by Ergun Ozbudun, 1976. Princeton University Press.

The Arabs, Israelis, and Kissinger: A Secret History of American Diplomacy in the Middle East, by Edward R.F. Sheehan, 1976. Reader's Digest Press.

Perception and Misperception in International Politics, by Robert Jervis, 1976. Princeton University Press.

Power and Interdependence, by Robert O. Keohane and Joseph S. Nye, Jr., 1977. Little, Brown & Co.

Soldiers in Politics: Military Coups and Governments, by Eric Nordlinger, 1977. Prentice-Hall.

The Military and Politics in Modern Times: On Professionals, Praetorians, and Revolutionary Soldiers, by Amos Perlmutter, 1977. Yale University Press.

Bankers and Borders: The Case of the American Banks in Britain, by Janet Kelly, 1977. Ballinger Publishing Co.

Shattered Peace: The Origins of the Cold War and the National Security State, by Daniel Yergin, 1977. Houghton Mifflin.

Storm Over the Multinationals: The Real Issues, by Raymond Vernon, 1977. Harvard University Press.

Political Generations and Political Development, ed. Richard J. Samuels, 1977. Lexington Books.

Cuba: Order and Revolution in the Twentieth Century, by Jorge I. Dominguez, 1978. Harvard University Press.

Raw Materials Investments and American Foreign Policy, by Stephen D. Krasner, 1978. Princeton University Press.

Commodity Conflict: The Political Economy of International Commodity Negotiations, by L.N. Rangarajan, 1978. Cornell University Press and Croom Helm (London).

Standing Guard: The Protection of Foreign Investment, by Charles Lipson, 1978. University of California Press.

Israel: Embattled Ally, by Nadav Safran, 1978. Harvard University Press.

HARVARD STUDIES IN INTERNATIONAL AFFAIRS*

[*Formerly Occasional Papers in International Affairs*]

*Available from Harvard University Center for International Affairs, 1737 Cambridge Street, Cambridge, Massachusetts 02138
†Out of print. Reprints may be ordered from AMS Press, Inc., 56 East 13th Street, New York, N.Y. 10003

†21. *Internal War and International Systems: Perspectives on Method,* by George A. Kelley and Linda B. Miller, 1969.

†22. *Migrants, Urban Poverty, and Instability in Developing Nations,* by Joan M. Nelson, 1969. 81 pp.

23. *Growth and Development in Pakistan, 1955-1969,* by Joseph J. Stern and Walter P. Falcon, 1970. 94 pp. $3.50.

24. *Higher Education in Developing Countries: A Select Bibliography,* by Philip G. Altbach, 1970. 118 pp. $4.50.

25. *Anatomy of Political Institutionalization: The Case of Israel and Some Comparative Analyses,* by Amos Perlmutter, 1970. 60 pp. $2.95.

†26. *The German Democratic Republic from the Sixties to the Seventies,* by Peter Christian Ludz, 1970. 100 pp.

27. *The Law in Political Integration: The Evolution and Integrative Implications of Regional Legal Processes in the European Community,* by Stuart A. Scheingold, 1971. 63 pp. $2.95.

28. *Psychological Dimensions of U.S.-Japanese Relations,* by Hiroshi Kitamura, 1971. 46 pp. $2.50.

29. *Conflict Regulation in Divided Societies,* by Eric A. Nordlinger, 1972. 142 pp. $4.95.

30. *Israel's Political-Military Doctrine,* by Michael I. Handel, 1973. 101 pp. $3.75.

31. *Italy, NATO, and the European Community: The Interplay of Foreign Policy and Domestic Politics,* by Primo Vannicelli, 1974. 67 + x pp. $3.75.

32. *The Choice of Technology in Developing Countries: Some Cautionary Tales,* by C. Peter Timmer, John W. Thomas, Louis T. Wells. Jr., and David Morawetz, 1975. 114 pp. $3.95.

33. *The International Role of the Communist Parties of Italy and France,* by Donald L.M. Blackmer and Annie Kriegel, 1975. 67 + x pp. $3.50.

34. *The Hazards of Peace: A European View of Detente,* by Juan Cassiers, 1976. 95 pp. $3.50.

35. *Oil and the Middle East War: Europe in the Energy Crisis,* by Robert J. Lieber, 1976. 75 + x pp. $3.45.

37. *Climatic Change and World Affairs,* by Crispin Tickell, 1977. 78 pp. $3.95.

38. *Conflict and Violence in Lebanon: Confrontation in the Middle East,* by Walid Khalidi, 1979. 180 pp. $12.95 cloth; $6.95 paper.

39. *Diplomatic Dispute: U.S. Conflict with Iran, Japan, and Mexico,* by Robert L. Paarlberg, Ed., Eul. Y. Park, and Donald L. Wyman, 1979. 173 pp. $11.95 cloth; $5.95 paper.

40. *Commandos and Politicians: Elite Military Units in Modern Democracies,* by Eliot A. Cohen, 1978. 136 pp. $8.95 cloth; $3.95 paper.

41. *Yellow Earth, Green Jade: Constants in Chinese Political Mores,* by Simon de Beaufort, 1979. 90 pp. $8.95 cloth; $3.95 paper.

42. *The Future of North America: Canada, the United States, and Quebec Nationalism,* Elliot J. Feldman and Neil Nevitte, Eds., 1979. 378 pp. $13.95 cloth; $6.95 paper.

091768